Guardrailing

"In *Guardrailing*, author Mike Bush delivers a soul-searching approach to building a successful business. Through a potent blend of practical wisdom and a checklist approach, this book empowers entrepreneurs to clarify their vision and stay focused on achieving meaningful success. It is an indispensable resource for any startup founder embarking on the exhilarating journey of entrepreneurship."

— BARBARA BRUECKNER SHPIZNER,
Food & Beverage Innovation Consultant, MATTSON

"I have been advising natural products companies for over 25 years, and I wish I could go back in time and give every one of them this book. Written by an industry veteran with a track record of success, it is chock full of great advice and clear action items to avoid so many of the obvious and not-so-obvious mistakes I have seen. It's an accessible and invaluable guide that will give readers an edge in this incredible but highly competitive industry."

— IVAN WASSERMAN,
Partner, Amin Wasserman Gurnani, LLP

"*Guardrailing* is a comprehensive and insightful guide for natural products entrepreneurs. It expertly navigates the industry's complexities, providing authentic strategies to guide your company toward achieving its goals. This book is a must-read for anyone looking to embark on or enhance their journey in the natural products sector."

— NATASHA DHAYAGUDE,
CEO and co-founder, Chinova Bioworks

"I have worked with Mike Bush on multiple projects in the natural products industry over the last several years, including the sale of Ganeden to Kerry. Mike is undoubtedly one of the most amazing people I have met in my long career. His leadership skills and communication skills are second to none."

— JIMMY BONNEAU,
Managing Director and Global Head of Consumer Health,
Rothschild & Co

"Job titles do not make an impact. The people behind them do, and Mike is a perfect example of this. He is a people-first leader who understands team building and how to help each person recognize their own superpowers. In his book, he teaches this influence to help make people feel successful, rewarded, and happy in their careers and lives."

— ELISETTE CARLSON,
Founder, SMACK! Media

"*Guardrailing* offers invaluable guidance for entrepreneurs seeking to steer their companies towards their destination while staying true to their values. It's a must-read for anyone looking to enhance their decision-making prowess and cultivate a culture of purpose-driven leadership."

— TODD BECKMAN,
CEO, Verb Biotics and Co-Founder, GoodBelly

"*Guardrailing* offers an understandable, practical, and empowering approach to building and growing a successful team and business. I wish I had these insights when I launched KeVita Drinks. Highly recommended!"

— CHAKRA EARTHSONG,
Founder, KeVita

"Mike's one of the few people in the industry who knows what it takes to turn innovations into ingredients and products that people not only love... but buy. He also understands what it's like to build a team driven by passion for the mission *and* results. He's been the guy I've turned to over the years for guidance on building my business. I wish I had this book years ago!"

— AFIF GHANNOUM,
CEO, Next Trillion Sciences,
Founder and Chairman, BIOHM Health

GUARD

RAILING

Authentically Guide Your
NATURAL
PRODUCTS
COMPANY
from SPARK
to SALE

Michael Bush

modern wisdom
PRESS

Modern Wisdom Press

Crestone, Colorado, USA

www.modernwisdompress.com

ISBN: 978-1-951692-41-4 (paperback), 978-1-951692-42-1 (epub)

DISCLAIMER

To those who have come before us
to build the natural products industry and
those who will follow to make the world
a better, healthier, and happier place.

Contents

Foreword 1

Introduction. 5

Chapter 1: Guardrailing Your Way to Success. 9

Chapter 2: Origin Story 25

Chapter 3: Guardrailing in Practice 41

Chapter 4: Start with Your Destination in Mind 55

Chapter 5: Create Your Business Roadmap. 69

Chapter 6: Fundraising 85

Chapter 7: Building a Team 101

Chapter 8: Avoid Unnecessary Science Detours 117

Chapter 9: Continuous Assessment 127

Chapter 10: Destination Reached—The Sale 139

Chapter 11: That's a Wrap!. 153

About the Author. 156

Acknowledgments 158

Thank You 159

FOREWORD

When Mike approached me to write the foreword of his new book, I was flattered, to say the least.

Reading Mike's book reminded me of my first week at Round-Table Healthcare Partners, a prominent health and wellness-focused private equity firm, back in the fall of 2007. I was in my late twenties and was so excited to have found my dream career at such a highly regarded private equity firm. I was ready to set the world on fire. That week, one of the founding partners imparted a valuable lesson: "Your decisions should prioritize doing right by employees and customers, and only then will the financial rewards follow."

This ethos mirrors the fundamental principles you'll learn about in this book. Mike's Guardrailing philosophy is simple yet profound—the synergy between knowing your destination and doing good. It's tempting to sacrifice the latter in pursuit of the former, but my tenure at RoundTable demonstrated that success is best achieved by upholding both principles unwaveringly.

Now a retired managing partner at RoundTable, I see a bit of myself in Mike and imagine if you're a trailblazer or a self-described misfit, you might, too. As he humorously describes, we are both oddballs (though I'd argue I'm slightly more aesthetically pleasing), marching to the beat of our own drums—or, in his case, guitar. We also share very similar views on business building and value creation for shareholders while also "doing Good" for the communities in which we serve.

Building businesses and creating shareholder value starts and ends with building the right relationships with the right people. You could be investing or operating in the highest growth, most profitable market, but if you do not have the right leaders at the top of the organization creating a positive culture, empowering employees, and prioritizing strategic objectives, you are climbing up an icy hill.

During my tenure at RoundTable, I relied on a self-deprecating sense of humor to connect with others on a personal level and build lasting relationships based upon a strong foundation of trust. I wanted to break down the "business formality wall" as quickly as possible to get to know folks personally to see if we could work together. I'm sure lots of colleagues thought of me as a bit of an oddball, but the relationships that I built with the leaders of our portfolio companies played a crucial role in overcoming challenging obstacles and creating significant shareholder value.

I first met Mike when RoundTable endeavored to acquire Mike's business, Ganeden, through one of our portfolio companies. Although we lost the bid to a multinational buyer, our brief intersection left a lasting impression.

At Ganeden, Mike blazed trails and set tables for the gut health industry. While he touches on this in his book, it is worth reiterating here: breaking into the market of spore-forming probiotics in the food and beverage industry was no easy feat due to various regulatory, safety, and clinical hurdles. Mike's success stemmed from his unorthodox approach and his ability to innovate free from industry predispositions. Central to his achievements were the core principles of Guardrailing:

defining a precise Destination and prioritizing ethical practices (i.e. "doing Good").

Mike and his team at Ganeden didn't just enter a market; they birthed a new one. This is akin to an entrepreneur launching a groundbreaking product or service. I can vouch for Mike's credentials and experiences in the natural products industry without hesitation. He's navigated the uncertainties and challenges of pivoting a business by defining a brand-new market in uncharted territory and emerged triumphant.

In the chapters ahead, you'll discover that by embracing the core principles of Guardrailing, your decision-making will become increasingly intuitive and guided by a steadfast North Star. Crucially, integrating these principles ensures the avoidance of shortcuts and enhances the likelihood of building a business with enduring value.

As you embark on your own entrepreneurial journey, may the experiences and wisdom Mike shares in the pages ahead help illuminate your path to success. When your compass is ultimately oriented toward "doing Good," the Guardrailing approach will empower you to forge a business that thrives ethically and sustainably, guiding you toward the destination of your dreams.

—Andrew B. Hochman
Former Managing Partner (Retired)
at RoundTable Healthcare Partners

Introduction

I'm an awkward fit in the business world. To be honest, it could be argued that I'm an odd fit in the world in general. More on that as you start reading through these pages. But the reason I mention being a kind of misfit here, in the Introduction, is that I want you to know why I wrote this book.

I have found that an outsider's gaze can offer a way of re-envisioning common perspectives on a subject. My own way of experiencing the business world has empowered me with a unique perspective on traditional approaches to launching, building, and selling a company. And what in my earlier life seemed like disadvantages have shown themselves to be assets.

While I have very limited formal education and even less classical training, I do know people. And I know how to build a winning team while putting processes in place to help them perform at their absolute best. These are skills I want to impart to you. Most importantly, through close observation of the companies I've served, I have devised an approach to generating and cultivating a business that flies in the face of traditional methods. The approach I have developed empowers leaders to think creatively, to engage their passion and their imagination, and to dispense with those rigid, cut-and-paste notions about how to approach the creation of value in a company.

What I am describing is Guardrailing, a method of inquiry that is immensely flexible and adaptable while keeping a company on course both strategically and ethically.

This approach has served me quite well, both in my own business endeavors and in the work I have done as a consultant supporting innovators, executives, aspiring CEOs, and visionaries as they dive into their entrepreneurial efforts. And now I want to expand the reach of Guardrailing by offering it to you.

Archimedes said, "Give me a lever long enough and a fulcrum on which to place it, and I shall move the world." I have always said, "Give me a smart, talented team of oddballs with people skills and a good attitude, and we can achieve anything." In my last journey down this path, my team of oddballs (and I mean that in the most loving way possible) built and grew a business that was sold for over $150 million. How about a shout-out to the misfits?

Writing this book has been a journey. I have had to look back at what worked and what failed, what resonated with customers and what turned them off. Ultimately, this book is an encapsulation of my decades of experience learning from some of the best (and worst) and shaping my own vision—one that I believe may be exactly what you need.

I found my people in the natural products industry, and so in some ways this book is an ode to the natural products industry and those who participate in it and do so with a mission to change the world. But it is also a book for absolutely anyone launching a business, no matter the field. It's about a decision-making and leadership system that allows individuals to be individuals while focusing on collectively beneficial goals. It is written for the open-minded entrepreneur looking for a roadmap to success. It is written for the struggling manager who knows that there is a solution to her challenge, but her current way of acting and thinking is not working. It is written for anyone who wants to inspire teams to be great, to think creatively, and to act intentionally. Ultimately, this book is intended to demonstrate how a simple approach to leadership and decision-making can shape and direct the future of an organization.

Being an oddball, I have found, is in fact my superpower. It may also be yours. Perhaps you find yourself confused or frustrated by the traditional guidance offered in academic settings or business manuals. Maybe those ideas have aligned with your thinking in some ways but absolutely not in others. Maybe you don't have a handle on how to accomplish this mammoth task: to make a business manifest, flourish, and become ready for sale. If you are feeling like an odd match for the entrepreneurial or solopreneurial arena yourself, you're not alone. Your uniqueness may be your strength. I bet it is. And this is your book.

CHAPTER 1

Guardrailing Your Way to Success

Sometimes, some of the best-conceived plans require pivots, adaptations, and alterations based on the learning, the market, target market, psychographic, demographic, usage, and occasion.

—Bill Moses, Cofounder & CEO of Kevita

I hit the refresh button over and over until it happened: The numbers on the screen changed, and my checking account balance increased by several million dollars. Thanks to a bit of luck and a massive amount of focused, demanding work, the day had finally come. Ganeden's success as a global probiotic innovator was spilling from margin to margin and blowing my mind.

Ganeden's investors, employees, and their families benefited from a journey that was focused and well executed. The day after I achieved this milestone, I was surprised that I woke up feeling like the same person who had been on this long and thrilling journey, but with the profound sense of accomplishment that comes from reaching a "Destination" exactly as planned.

I had come to the end of my journey with Ganeden and was stunned by the fruits of our collective labor as they unfurled across my laptop screen. And it was while I was at Ganeden that

I sharpened the leadership approach that got the company to this point—and I would take that approach with me to serve the dozens of consulting clients that followed. But I didn't start out imagining that I'd achieve this success. I began with an innovative idea and a lot of passion and a big fat hope that things would pan out!

I suspect you and I are cut from the same cloth. You are beginning with a dream. You may have come up with a product or a service that no one in your industry has considered, and you know that the concept that's been finding its shape in your mind will help people. After all, doing meaningful good is the reason you were attracted to this field in the first place.

Do I have it right?

You are ready to build a business that will take this vision you've mulled over and diagrammed and woken up a hundred nights at 2 a.m. to refine in your notes and deliver that business into a world that needs it. You want to create a company that produces it, grow that company until it is functionally and fiscally strong, and sell to a purchaser that will carry on your work ethically.

It's a worthy vision.

But you've got a problem. *That's why you picked up this book.*

Whether you've had years of experience launching startups or you're a total newbie to this territory, your problem is that you don't have a method for making the choices necessary to get you to your goal. You don't have a decision-making process.

You need help.

How do I know this? I was in your shoes. Traditional business approaches failed me. So, I developed a method that would work in the real world to guide me to success. Once the sparkly dust settled, I saw that what worked in my case could be applied to businesses of all kinds, especially within the natural products world. It became my dream and my mission to help visionary startups make their way from a glimmering notion of a company to a triumphant exit—using the means of decision-making I had designed, the method that stunned me with its success. This book is my offering to those big thinkers who are hungry to manifest their ideas and don't want to waste time using outdated approaches. This book is my hand reaching toward yours as you take the leap.

On-Ramp to Success

Let's back up to before I'd ever heard the name "Ganeden."

I was gonna do it—I was gonna be the best business consultant the world had ever seen. I was thirty-five years old and had just started consulting. I had achieved some success in business over the years, and it was time to share my brilliance with the world.

One of my first clients wanted me to find ways to increase revenue and to come up with a plan to incentivize their company's employees to increase sales. I worked sixteen-hour days to develop a system and metrics by which each sales representative would be measured and given a quota for calls, emails, and revenue. Theoretically, profits would improve as the processes and measurements were implemented, and as a result, the sales team members would increase their earnings.

But theory be damned—the entire exercise was a disaster. Highly productive sales team members only met the bare minimum requirements that were defined in the program, while underperformers simply continued to underperform. To make matters worse, the increased workload caused them to spend less time working with their existing customers in order to focus on finding new ones, ultimately leading to lost business and no significant increase in revenue.

It's no surprise my contract wasn't renewed. That job was a grand failure, and it was all my fault. But I wasn't alone in the mistakes I made—companies everywhere were making the same ones, and still are: erratic decisions based on old business models.

Clearly, the time had come to swipe away the cobwebs of outdated and cumbersome business practices. This was true then, and it's still true today. Companies need a simple but effective method to successfully guide their progress, from founding to exit.

The method: Guardrailing.

What Is Guardrailing?

The launching and development of every business requires making decisions—lots and lots of them. Even if you are at the very beginning of your company's arc, you have no doubt encountered this phenomenon. Unless an emerging business has a method in place for encountering crossroads and determining which direction to take, the decision-making process is likely to be confusing, stressful, and potentially even disastrous.

Guardrailing is a method of inquiry. It lifts the fog of confusion by providing a simple set of guidelines, or "guardrails," that can—and should—be applied to every choice a company makes, from the smallest to the most immense.

Using Guardrailing, a business can rest assured that its operational decisions align with its overarching goals. The business avoids chaos and achieves clarity, and each day, the work is done with the entire team's focus on the same common aims.

Guardrailing will take you from the murky hope of achieving your goal to the concrete assurance of knowing how to get there.

The Two Core Principles of Guardrailing: Destination and Good

When using Guardrailing, a company relies on two essential questions to navigate any business decision:

1.   Does this decision move you toward your **Destination**?
2.   Is it a **Good** decision?

This may seem like a simple strategy, but simple can be precisely what you need. And believe me, it works. I have found, in the dozens of companies I have served as a consultant, that basing the company's decision-making on these two considerations leads them to their end goal and keeps them from straying into disaster. This can be your journey, too.

Let's look at each of the principles more closely.

Destination

If we use the analogy of a road trip, Guardrailing centers around the process of determining a precise Destination (i.e., Goal), and then working backward to map a route to that Destination. That path, much like a meandering road trip, may take unexpected turns. But focusing on your Destination ensures you ultimately stay on course. Establishing your Destination, your ultimate objective, is a universal necessity for success.

I have done well in this industry. The key to my success and the success of my clients is knowing the Destination before all else. Without a Destination, you can spend years spinning your wheels, or worse, looking up at the road from the bottom of that proverbial ditch. With your Destination in sight, you will remain aimed at the spot on the horizon where you want to arrive resourced, energized, and ready for your desired exit.

Good

Knowing your Destination is crucial, and this book will dive deeply into that approach. But Guardrailing is more than just a mechanism for reaching your end goal successfully. It includes a nuanced layer of decision-making that incorporates your company's concerns around ethical, cultural, and long-term implications. I refer to this layer as Good.

A "Good decision" is one that not only serves the immediate objective, but also aligns with the broader values of the individual and business. You will never regret making that decision. For this reason, considering every decision's Goodness is as important as considering each decision's ability to get you to your Destination. I passionately believe that the Good decision is an ethical one that benefits all.

I have heard people, executives, and even CEOs say that to be successful in business, you must be ruthless, take no prisoners, have a maniacal focus on urgency, and the list goes on and on.

But winning at all costs is a recipe for disaster. Without ethically grounded decisions at the heart of a business, the success of a few people may very well leave all sorts of devastation in its wake. Without weighing the Goodness of a decision, you are only looking at half of a very important equation.

Destination + Goodness = Success.

Meanwhile,

Destination – Goodness = Failure.

It's that simple.

Outside of those who are out to help no one but themselves (which I've met plenty of over my years in business), I believe that the desire to make ethical choices tends to be pretty universal from the perspective of those in the natural products industry. Yet I am often shocked at how hard it is for businesses to clearly identify their values. Those values can be as simple as "do no harm" or as complex as "ensure that our products and services benefit all living beings and the environment while leaving the world a better place than we found it." "Doing Good" means just that: doing all you can to ensure that no activity in your business—from your raw materials and supply chain to the way you handle employee benefits—causes undue harm to anyone or anything. Again, it's simple, but it requires constant mindful consideration.

Decisions Make or Break Your Business

You may be wondering why I put so much emphasis on decisions. Consider for a moment what is a business other than the result of decisions. What will you sell and to whom? Should the product formula be changed? Should you hire Ava or make the tough call to let Dave go? Every decision shapes the entity a business becomes.

Guardrailing keeps a company's decision-making on track and aimed toward its Destination. This commonsense approach, guided by those two fundamental principles, informs and elevates your company's decision-making.

My clients, from wide-eyed newcomers to industry veterans, seek my help in making decisions. Often, they don't know what choices need to be made, or even exactly where they are headed. But if you are aiming to launch and ultimately sell a successful business in the natural products industry, I bet these examples of client questions will sound familiar:

- "How can we accelerate growth?"
- "What can we do to get our employees to be more productive?"
- "How can we get our ingredient or product to market more quickly?"
- "We are getting a lot of inquiries about selling our company, but I'm not sure we are ready yet. What should we do to prepare?"
- "We need to raise money, but venture money isn't as easy to come by as it used to be. How can we fundraise?"
- "What's the best way to reduce turnover?"
- "How can I avoid micromanaging?"

Through years of leading businesses and coaching, I've found that by simply *changing how decisions are made* can be the key.

Despite what many of us were taught, when it comes to a business, decision-making processes do not always benefit from flow charts. Rather, common sense and guiding principles lead us, with ethical grounding, to an ultimate Destination. As with most of life, the solution is often straightforward but requires a shift in mindset—in this case, a shift to Guardrailing.

Your Particular Destination: Sale

In this book, the assumed Destination is the ultimate sale of the company you've built, and there are two reasons for that. First, it is a common exit opportunity for companies in the natural products space, and second, it is a path that is underexplored in business literature. So, the following chapters are aimed at helping your company make the decisions that will help you reach that goal.

Note: Guardrailing works well regardless of the Destination (so long as the Destination is clearly defined). Whether building a business to sell or to grow and provide resources for future generations, it still benefits from Guardrailing.

My expertise lies in the journey to sale. Over my thirty-plus-year career in the natural products, healthcare service, bioinformatics, and medical device industries, I have focused on working with and for companies that were started with the objective of selling the business to provide a return for investors. And while each industry has its own unique characteristics that add complexity to the process, the decision-making process that leads us toward our ultimate Destination is consistent.

Guardrailing as a Broad Practice

Decisions made through Guardrailing apply to every aspect of your business (and life—but for the purposes of this book, we will focus on business). You can use this same decision-making methodology when it comes to hiring people, buying capital equipment, advertising, going to trade shows, travel, new product launches, intellectual property, territory expansion, product enhancements, the types of customers you work with, and the list goes on and on.

And unlike traditional management theory, Guardrailing is effective for virtually any organization. Solopreneurs, B2B (Business to Business) product and service providers, D2C (Direct to Consumer) and brick and mortar CPG (Consumer Packaged Goods) businesses, private equity–and venture capital–backed companies, and even large public companies can all benefit from using Guardrails. Guardrailing offers a methodical way of navigating the complex landscape of choices that define the path of a business, because it is a decision-making method rather than a set of fixed rules.

As you will see in the coming pages, this is not a book about business theory, new ways of doing things, or some woo-woo approach to managing that involves drum circles at lunch. It is about a process that offers an intuitive approach to designing, growing, and making a wildly successful exit *while* truly supporting staff, benefiting the planet, and operating with ethics at the core of your business.

Natural Products and the Wider World of Business

The natural products industry is perfect for this straightforward approach. Guardrailing ensures you build a team that is along for the ride for more reasons than simply receiving a paycheck. Employees in a business guided by Guardrailing want to make the world a better place, and they know they can do it more effectively as part of a team than they may be able to manage individually.

I have been working in the natural products industry for close to two decades. I have found my people in this industry—fellow visionaries with outsider sensibilities who care about the impact of the work they are doing. This is the community I identify with and serve. And the examples you'll find me discussing in these pages come primarily from my experience working with people in the natural products industry.

Again, though, the concepts throughout this book are applicable to leaders working in all areas of the business world. No matter your focus, if you are launching a company you intend to sell, you would do well to utilize Guardrailing. Many more conventional companies will find the approach not just effective, but also refreshing—hopefully adding a dash of fun to the work. Meanwhile, natural products businesses may find that the method comfortably aligns with their culture. However, no matter what industry a company is inhabiting, the same two primary principles apply as decision-making guidelines: *Destination* first, and the ethic of *Good*.

What Guardrailing *Isn't*

Guardrailing isn't your parents' business model. The way we (should) hire, manage, train, lead, supply, etc. in the twenty-first century, especially post-pandemic, is far removed from how we managed in the 1950s, but many companies are still structured and operated as if they were stuck back in time. Strict reporting hierarchies, siloed business units, bloated senior management teams, archaic comp plans, and HR-driven policies and procedures choke countless companies. If you peer through the window, you're likely to see desperate leadership squinting back, seeking solutions to internal problems.

In sharp contrast to traditional management and leadership approaches—where adherence to corporate policies, procedures, and a strict chain of command is the norm—Guardrailing allows for the members of your team to behave authentically. It enables them to produce value for the company while remaining true to the *person* you hired in the first place. I cannot tell you how many times I have seen great people brought into organizations because of certain skill sets or personal attributes, only to watch the very characteristics that were pivotal in the hiring process get squashed by management to ensure that the organizational status quo is not upset. We hire people—or *should* hire people—based on their ability to use their individual talents to support the journey of the company.

Plans guided by traditional management theory are typically rigid and force the business to adjust (sometimes with great force) to fit the model, while the beauty of plans guided by Guardrails is that they are flexible and able to be adapted on the fly.

That's also the fun.

If I'd Known Then...

Back when I was that thirty-five-year-old consultant, before I'd devised the system that would propel Ganeden forward and change the course of my career, Guardrails would have prevented my bad decisions. They would have made certain the client's revenue was protected while new revenue was generated from existing clients. And Guardrails would have ensured that when new clients were brought on, there were already systems in place so they were happily served by a company able to meet their needs.

But life calls on us to grow and change, and I'm sure that's been your experience as well. Back then, I didn't know what I know now, and I surely didn't have the breadth of insight and experience that I am so excited to share with you in these pages. My hope is to save you a lot of trouble, money, time, and stress by offering you what I've learned myself over the years.

I didn't invent the idea of using guardrails in general, but I believe the concept of Guardrailing is unique to my way of working, managing, leading, or whatever you want to call it. I look at it as a way to use two simple questions to make virtually any decision. So long as we ask those two basic questions when evaluating a situation, it is hard to find an instance where Guardrailing doesn't work.

Early in my career, though I was working toward this approach, I didn't have a firm grasp of it. That didn't come until I narrowed the process down to two basic questions. Originally, I had flowcharts and index cards, took polls, and used a good bit of gut feeling. I found that the more variables there were in the decision-making process, the more convoluted the answer was. Yet the desired answer is at its core binary: *yes* or *no*. In other words, do you go forward with the decision or not?

If you use Guardrailing to guide the launch of your business and prepare it for an ultimate sale, you are likely to avoid the potholes, speedbumps, and even catastrophic cliff dives so many startups can't help but encounter. This book is a manual for your empowerment, and it may wind up being the key to your success.

I know that this method of inquiry invites individuals to be individuals while cultivating teams and cultures that thrive. And I know that with Guardrailing, a glimmer of an idea can be turned into a spectacular business success. I've done it, and I've witnessed it. I have used the techniques in this book to help others realize their dreams, transforming a concept into a new life for themselves and all the fortunate souls they involve along the way. So, welcome to my world—a world I want to extend to you.

How to Use This Book

If you are like most people aiming to start or grow a business, some concepts in this volume may seem unfamiliar. That's because this approach operates in direct contradiction to traditional business training. So, I encourage you to pay careful attention to the early chapters that explain and illustrate Guardrailing, its principles, and its ideas.

The book presents Guardrailing in practice, with each chapter focused on a different area where this decision-making method can be used. These chapters will cover areas you may have encountered already in the emerging stage of your company, as well as concerns that you may face down the line. Threaded throughout are personal reflections rooted in my experience with consulting clients. I also share insights from my work with Ganeden, since I learned so much from that professional trek, and my history there informs a great deal of the guidance I offer clients today. All of what you are about to read is designed to offer you clarity about how to engage Guardrailing strategies to successfully navigate each challenge that emerges.

And Last: How to Approach the Reflection Questions

At the end of each chapter, I have posed questions to help you integrate and begin to implement the ideas you have read. Try keeping a notebook and pen—or a tablet if you prefer a screen—near this book. As the end-of-chapter questions arise, you might meditate for a moment on the issues they bring up, or you might just attack the page with gusto, responding to the queries. Either way, I hope these brief bits of personal application will help translate big-picture concepts down to the practical realities of your life, as you work toward your business's success.

CHAPTER 2

Origin Story

Be the change you wish to see in the world.

—Mahatma Gandhi

I want you to know how the theories and strategies in this book came to be. To understand why these concepts are worth your consideration, you deserve a sense of their evolution. Also, in my work as a consultant with venture-backed businesses, I am invariably asked to tell my professional "origin story" with the probiotic ingredient innovator Ganeden Biotech, since it can be a source of inspiration and lessons learned. So, this chapter is really the story of how Guardrailing came to be, braided together with my experience at Ganeden.

Guardrailing was not birthed during my time with Ganeden. The concept had been knocking around in my mind over the years. But my work with Ganeden sure gave it a chance to spread its wings. The responsibility I held, along with the constant challenge of high-stakes decision-making, required an approach that would keep me on track and keep me ethically grounded—and prevent me from losing my mind!

Once I'd established myself with the Ganeden success, potential clients began coming out of the woodwork. People wanted to know how we'd done it and how they could do something

similar. It was thrilling to have a substantial success to draw from at that point, along with a methodology (Guardrailing, of course) that I could offer to businesses to help them as they moved forward.

In sharing my history, I want you to recognize that I *get* you—and I've *got* you. I care that your business makes it, and it matters to me that you and your team reach the finish line with the right product or service in a way that fulfills both your dreams and your values.

So, in these next pages, you'll get the narrative behind the guidance, and a feel for the person behind the words. And I hope you'll feel a connection with me, because ultimately, we operate in the same community. We share the same orientation. Or, to put it another way, I have a feeling we're part of the same club.

Confession

I am not in any way your typical success story. I did not graduate with my bachelor's degree until I was in my late thirties. I had no exposure whatsoever to the world of high finance. I've been divorced twice. I grew up *very* lower middle class. As a bonus, I have struggled my entire life with severe ADHD, anxiety, depression, and Tourette's syndrome. And if you passed me on the street, you might never look at me and think "Well there's your typical CEO." I have well over a dozen tattoos and own just one single suit.

That's me at first glance.

I have always been a work in progress. Maybe you'd say the same about yourself. I haven't always been thoughtful in my communications. I've been a bad manager who yelled and berated. Much of my success can be attributed to my ability to work for extended periods of time with little rest. This, of course, has been a mixed blessing. At certain points in my career, I labored and traveled to such extremes that my family paid the price: having an absentee spouse and parent.

But I have always *known* I was a work in progress. And, perhaps like you, I have tried very hard to become a better person. An avid explorer of ways to improve myself and the world around me, I drive people crazy by obsessing over technology solutions and "biohacking" that may (or may not) somehow advance my life. I meditate regularly, and my love for that practice called me to become a certified meditation instructor. Over the years I have attended meditation retreats, innovation summits, and ultimately the real game changers, the Hoffman Process and The Modern Elder Academy (see online resources for more information—then sign up to attend!). On my home screen, a calendar shows (if I live to the randomly selected age of ninety) how many days I have left in this life.

In other words, I am at once perpetually imperfect and driven each day to be a better version of my messy, human self. I'm guessing the same is true of you.

The Birth of This Method

At the age of nineteen, the previously described atypical, aspiring business professional launched his career. I started out in healthcare, an industry ruled by insurance reimbursement yet managed by individuals who entered the field with a common mission of caring for patients. The people I met who were running the departments were overworked and burdened by productivity measurements, documentation for billing, and struggles in finding and retaining staff. The executives were often as overwhelmed, and their overwhelm was typically due to budgetary constraints or the constant demands to do more with less and less. There seemed to be little focus on strategy, growth, or process improvement outside of enhancing the productivity of the staff.

I once did a weeklong time study of a department and monitored the flow of the work and how the staff interacted with each other, the tasks they were supposed to accomplish, and where efficiency could be increased. At the end of the week, I had a massive log of activities—and when I sat down and worked through it all, I found that the productivity goals were simply too high for the staff to accomplish effectively. I came away with two suggestions: (1) Move the processing entryway closer to the surgical hallway, so the staff doesn't have to move surgical trays all the way across the department twice. And (2) Hire two more people. But of course, I was hired because the administrators were looking for cost-cutting measures, so they didn't see my recommendations—and particularly my second recommendation, the one that would have been the most effective—as viable options. Instead, they saw the time study— and my work as a time studier—as a flop.

"There has to be a better way to make decisions that benefit everyone," I thought, in the aftermath, and that got my wheels turning.

A few years down the line, I was working as the manager of a group of clinical engineers located across half a dozen hospitals all over the Great Lakes region. The primary purpose of our team was to ensure that the patient care equipment in these hospitals was working perfectly and was available when needed. The ultimate measure of success for a clinical engineering department is how they handle their portion of a hospital's accreditation process through the Joint Commission. Each hospital is on an inspection cycle, and we had to prepare for the inspections by compiling service and preventive maintenance records for the inspectors, managing the complete inventory of patient care equipment, and reporting on adverse events. It is a massive undertaking, and we were using a dozen different systems that worked separately to provide the required records.

One day I was sitting with the COO of one of those hospitals, discussing the upcoming inspection, and he mentioned how time-consuming it was to simply gather the data. "No matter what records we pull," he said, "the inspector always wants something different, and we look ridiculous running around trying to find the records." Mind you, this was in the early days of shared databases, and most everything was kept on paper in filing cabinets. Our company was using a software system that was capable of doing most of the heavy lifting, but it required heavy customization, and the initial work involved in setting up a system in an existing hospital was immense.

I went home with a list of commonly asked questions posed by inspectors from past audits. While the requests were different, the place where the data could be stored was the same. I sat down and spent the next several weeks modifying the database and standardizing our system to account for the inspectors' requests. Our team had an inspection coming up in a few months at a smaller hospital, so we went to work preparing for it by standardizing that hospital's data, and I drafted a few report templates with search options that allowed us to instantly pull any record on any piece of equipment at the touch of a button.

During an accreditation inspection, we faced the biggest test of inspection—find random pieces of equipment in the hospital and show full histories. We were resourced in a brand-new way. With the updated database, we were able to instantly print the record—which included the location of the device, so we could lead the inspector directly to the device and match the information. A process that typically took a full day was completed in three hours. When we were finished, the inspector commented on how fantastic it was to see equipment care and systems prioritized.

Nationwide, we had hundreds of hospitals to take care of, so setting standards and developing easy-to-use processes was key. Our company became known as the premier provider of medical device asset management in the US. We ultimately sold that company to GE Medical Systems, and it became the leader in providing outsourced clinical engineering services to healthcare providers in the US.

This foray into decision modeling evolved over time into what is now the Guardrailing system.

Fast Forward to Ganeden

A few decades and a few million hard-fought lessons later, I was hired by Ganeden Biotech in 2006 as a consultant. I was charged with determining what other uses of their ingredients were viable outside of the consumer products that they were already selling. After reviewing the science and the market opportunities, I produced a summary and suggested to the CEO that their ingredient might be perfect for foods, beverages, supplements, and companion animal and livestock products. A few weeks later, we reviewed my market overview, and the CEO excitedly said that although these sounded like great opportunities, they did not have anyone to explore them—so he asked if I would like to join as an employee. I jumped at the chance and launched a new division of the business we called Ganeden Labs. I hit the ground running with a business pursuit that would radically change my life.

The company was already selling their patented probiotic through a line of consumer products marketed under the Digestive Advantage brand, which was distributed through tens of thousands of retail stores throughout the United States. But the real growth in the probiotic industry was in the food and beverage space, as the supplement space had become more mature, and consumers were looking for ways to consume probiotics outside of the traditional capsules or tablets. With that information in hand, we established the patented probiotic as GRAS ("Generally Regarded as Safe") by FDA standards and began working with food and beverage companies around the country to explore potential products.

There was one huge hurdle, though: the organism we were selling was from the genus *Bacillus* (now renamed *Weizmannia*). If you don't know what that means, you're not alone—most people have no idea. In short, it's a group of bacteria that includes, among other things, two species that are harmful to humans:

one causes food poisoning and the other causes anthrax. So, although the specific organism we were working with was safe and in fact beneficial to humans, there was understandably some hesitation to use it in a food manufacturing facility!

Since I had no experience in that space at the time, I made an appointment with the head of the food science department at a major university to discuss the plan to integrate our organism into food and beverage products. "Son, if you can convince one food or beverage manufacturer to bring this organism into their plant on purpose, I'll buy you lunch," said the elderly professor. "I've been teaching my students to keep *Bacillus* spores out of food plants for decades, and I can't image bringing one into a plant intentionally."

As I made the dejected ride home, I thought about my options and how I was going to explain to the CEO that this expert in our target industry had said that our business idea is pointless. But then again, we had data that supported the safety and efficacy of the organism, knew exactly what it would take to get the organism to grow, and felt confident that in controlled environments, there would be little chance of any sort of contamination.

I spent the next several months meeting with food and beverage manufacturers around the country, and repeatedly was met with constant rejection due to the spore-forming nature of the organism, which meant that it could spread very easily. Eventually, I met a man with a startup food company and a never-say-no attitude, and he wanted to be the first person to include a probiotic in a shelf-stable nutrition bar. So, we set out to find a contract manufacturer who would make the bar with our organism included. Fortunately, the man knew a couple of manufacturers who might be willing to try the ingredient.

After a brief period of testing, we found that the organism was extremely easy to incorporate into the bars and swabs of the manufacturing facility indicated that there was no cross-contamination. It turned out that the organism was exceptionally easy to control in the manufacturing environment because it was a dormant spore and needed unique environmental conditions to grow. We were even able to perform accelerated shelf-life testing on the products without any degradation of the organism. Within six months, the product was ready to launch.

Expo West 2008 saw the first release of a product containing what was officially called GanedenBC^{30} (now known as BC^{30}). We announced the launch to the media before the trade show, as our partner was launching several flavors of bars. They were met with good reception by a variety of retailers who wanted to carry the bars—and more surprisingly, there was also a great deal of interest from other companies selling bars and similar products.

When I returned from Expo West, there was a greeting card sitting on my desk. I opened it to find a short, surprising message—one from the professor I had consulted about the project, several years prior. He said, "You made me eat my words—now have lunch on me. Congratulations!"

Some say that ignorance is bliss. In this instance of ignorance, it truly was. I did not come from the food industry, so I did not know that there were strains of *Bacillus* that were food contamination organisms (or worse, deadly pathogens), and I was not aware that, due to their frail nature, probiotics were typically limited to refrigerated foods or supplements. But I did know that the data surrounding BC^{30} indicated that there was a huge market opportunity around shelf-stable, probiotic products.

As I built a team, I focused on individuals from outside of the natural products industry—and in particular, individuals with no experience selling food ingredients, supplement ingredients, or probiotics. This focus let me find people who did not have preconceived notions about what could or should be done—so those preconceived notions couldn't get in the way of figuring out what we could do.

The investors decided to sell Ganeden's consumer products business in 2012 to focus exclusively on the ingredient business. The consumer products business required a tremendous amount of cash to support the products at retail, while the ingredient business required little marketing spend and produced much higher margins.

Ganeden Labs eventually became simply Ganeden, and as co-founder of the ingredient business, I operated Ganeden under the principles that you'll be learning about in this book. The ingredient business grew at a remarkable pace, and our small team developed into a team of over thirty individuals who felt far more like family than work associates.

The organization was run using Guardrails, not generic policies and procedures, so its decisions were ethically driven rather than financially driven, and it operated as a team, with individual contributors playing unique and vital roles in the ultimate success of the business. The day the ingredient business was founded, we set a goal of selling the ingredient business for the highest possible value, while at the same time providing an ingredient that could improve the lives of consumers around the world. I was blessed to have had the autonomy to run Ganeden Labs separately from the consumer products group, and to hire individuals who were excited to join me on this adventure.

And it truly was an adventure. We went from a half dozen products in the market in 2008 to over one thousand products sold in over seventy countries in 2017. And the success—which stunned me no less than it delighted my colleagues—continued after that.

The remarkable arc that Ganeden went through has given me resounding faith that the ember of the right idea can be fanned into a big, glorious flame of success, if the leaders taking it forward rely on a solid decision-making method. It's what makes me believe in you, if you're launching a business on a hunch that won't leave you alone—a sharp idea, a gut sense of potential—even if you don't yet know the context for your concept. That nagging hunch can be the spark that becomes your unique and dazzling contribution. Your creative thinking starts it all, and it's worth honoring.

A Shout-Out to Our Naturals Niche . . .

You know all those traits I mentioned earlier that kept me awkwardly outside the norm? I didn't know it during the early years, but a wonderfully wild business culture awaited me. I was going to encounter a universe of oddballs who cared very little about typical business mores and cared deeply about their contributions to this world.

My introduction to the "real" natural products community was at Expo West in 2007. As I walked the floor, I noticed that the people, the way they dressed, the smells, the energy—everything—was vastly different from the healthcare, biotech, and bioinformatics conferences I was used to. The only attendees dressed in what would be considered business attire were the "ingredient people," as they are called by the industry insiders. Everyone else seemed to be attending an event that was part coming-out party (new product launches were everywhere) and part family reunion (everyone knew everyone). There were almost fifty thousand people in attendance, yet the event seemed intimate.

The natural products industry is full of characters. Some of the smartest people I have ever met work in this industry, and so do some of the most unique individuals I know. From PhDs to middle school dropouts, the natural products industry is chockfull of every type of individual you can imagine. My first Expo West was the first conference in my professional career where I felt at home. I was not surrounded by MDs or scientists working on billion-dollar pharmaceuticals, as I was used to. I found myself surrounded by tattooed, patchouli-wearing tree huggers who were proudly selling their products in hopes of changing the world. And I loved it. I did not have a stellar education, a background in the industry, or even a great appreciation for the naturals space—but I was used to being the "odd one," and suddenly, I had found my people.

It was there that I started meeting entrepreneurs who were running businesses driven by missions rather than business plans. Authenticity was the name of the game, and "corporate types" were looked at as trying to infiltrate the industry. After all, multinational CPG firms were taking a hard look at the industry, its loyal customers, and its high-margin, premium products. To them, it looked like an unlimited supply of opportunities for acquisitions, and natural products entrepreneurs were looked at often as easy marks for low-valuation takeovers.

What I found was an industry that was perfect for a less structured, more outcome-focused way of leading. The more people I met, the more I realized that mission was not just a statement to be hung on a conference room wall and ignored—it was the driving force behind some of the industry's biggest success stories. Companies like KeVita and Traditional Medicinals, to name just two, were out to do something special, and they kept their motivations at the center of their business, with the mission as the primary focus, rather than a spreadsheet. Sure, these companies were doing very well and growing rapidly, but they were doing so thanks to their maniacal focus on their missions. I loved what I saw, and I saw an opportunity to grow our business using the leadership system I had quietly been developing over the past decade.

An example of the authentic leadership that can be found in the naturals space is the founder of KeVita, a delightful woman named Chakra Earthsong. When first meeting her, you might think she was born in a yurt and wears exclusively tie-dyed clothing. But get to know Chakra, and you will find a person who is deeply passionate about the health, wellness, and lives of consumers, and knows that building a successful business is what allows her to feed that passion. She formulated the beverages that are enjoyed by millions of people today, and her passion was and continues to be serving others and helping people live their best lives. Chakra does not have an MBA from Wharton, but she does have common sense, a love for what she does, and a highly focused moral compass.

After over seventeen years in the industry, I honestly cannot imagine once again working anywhere but the natural products space or focusing on anything but the health and wellness of consumers around the world. The immense satisfaction that I have experienced over the years fills me with gratitude for an industry that is made up of passionate, hardworking individuals who are dedicated to the quality and efficacy of their products.

Of course, just like in any industry, there will always be rogues trying to capitalize on market opportunities—but I find these individuals rare, and their time in our industry short-lived.

And of course, I can't end this chapter without high-fiving my fellow expansive thinkers and one-suit owners. So, thank you to this incredible niche of outsiders. They have played a profound role in shaping my values and vision—and maybe they have done the same for you, as well.

And So...

Nowadays, I have found my place in the world. I consult with businesses that seek to make the world a better place. But as I help them make concrete use of the highly effective decision-making approach I devised and refined, I remain a complicated, convoluted work in progress. But when we stop evolving, we start to wither away. And the world doesn't need any more "good-enough" citizens taking up space. So, to you and me and the unusual, visionary, intent-on-growing people we draw to us as we forge our professional paths: We've got work to do. We've got worthy Destinations to reach, and we have Good to manifest along the way.

Reflection Questions

- What wonderfully unique/weird/oddball traits do you bring to the work you do today?

- Remembering your twists and turns, how has your personal journey led you to this current, exciting moment in your career?

CHAPTER 3

Guardrailing in Practice

*Connect your product with the people beyond your family and
friends, because that's where you'll really get the most honest
and true feedback.*

—Lilian Umurungi-Jung, Founder of Mumgry

So, now you have a sense of my circuitous path. You have
been properly introduced to me as this book's author, so
you know you're in good—if unconventional—hands. Now for
the good stuff. Let's turn our attention to how you can apply
Guardrailing as you develop your business.

It's time to invite your killer business or business idea into your
reading of this book. Call up its magic. As you move through
the following chapters, consider how you can apply the Guardrailing method specifically to the company you're getting off the
ground. No matter what kind of company you aim to launch,
Guardrailing is designed for you. It offers the force and flexibility you will need as you progress toward your end goal.

You've been introduced to the theory. Here, we'll look at the
practical application of Guardrails, so that we can make sure
they offer the guidance you'll need as you travel toward your
Destination.

How It Works

When setting Guardrails, we start with the end in mind. Once we've determined our end goal, we set off on the journey, putting action plans in place along the way to ensure a smooth passage. Sometimes the Guardrails will be wide to accommodate flexibility and innovation, while at other times, the Guardrails will be set close together to ensure that travelers remain safely on the path.

With Guardrailing, the same process—the same method of inquiry—applies to every decision your company makes. You run every situation through the same set of questions to ensure that you're on track. But depending on the specific issue at hand, you will refine the essential questions, making sure they precisely address what's at stake.

Here's a simple example. Consider the internal Guardrail questions a company might ask before engaging a contract manufacturer:

- Will this contract manufacturer propel us toward our Destination (our goal of eventual sale)? (Relatedly, will this company *understand* our goal?)

- Does this contract manufacturer have an ethical record that aligns with our principle of Good?

On a concrete level, the conclusions reached in response to these questions will point your company toward the right contract manufacturer. And by using this method of inquiry, your company can move through this decision-making process swiftly and efficiently, remaining directed toward your end goal.

Obviously, selecting a contract manufacturer is just one of many major decisions a company has to face. But it also falls into the category of the fairly predictable.

As you have likely come to recognize by now, businesses are organisms constantly in flux. Often, an unexpected concern arises. That's where Guardrailing comes in, with its ability to turn a nail-biting dilemma into a two-part thought process that yields a simple conclusion.

An example: I once had a customer call me on my cell phone late one Saturday afternoon. And yes—every customer, supplier, and team member has my number and knows they can call anytime the need arises. Anyway, that customer was freaking out—to put it lightly—that their frozen dairy dessert cartons, which were in the freezer section of a large national retailer, were puffing up, and some of the tops were popping off. He was concerned that the probiotics we provided to him for use in fortifying his frozen treats were growing in the product, producing gas, and making the cartons explode. Yep—I could see how that was a concern worth a call.

I tried to calm him down by telling him that first, our probiotic could not grow in freezing temperatures, and that second, I'd run to the store right that moment, buy the product, and get it to our lab for testing. I did indeed notice that some of the cartons were expanding and got them into our lab freezer immediately, so we could test them.

We could have simply confirmed that our probiotic was not causing the issue and left it at that, knowing that it was not the fault of our company or product. But using Guardrailing,

I considered the options. Question one: Does resolving this issue get us closer to our Destination? The answer of course is *yes*, delighted customers with products on store shelves add value to our company, therefore moving us closer to our Destination. Question two: Would resolving this problem be Good? Would determining the cause of the issue, regardless of fault, and hopefully finding a solution, support our customer? Of course, the answer was *yes* again. This poor guy was an entrepreneur, and a product quality issue could destroy his business.

With Guardrails firmly in place in response to this unanticipated challenge, we called in one of our scientists to determine what was growing in the product. After a few days of incubation and testing the organisms found in the product, we identified a strain of harmless bacteria that naturally grows on the shells of certain nuts. To kill this organism, the nuts needed to be heated at a slightly higher temperature than our customer's company was using.

Four days after the frantic call, we had identified the step in his manufacturing process where the heat could be added, and the customer was able to refine the manufacturing process and replace all of the units that were in stores nationwide without much fuss. Oh, and we did all of the testing and identification at no cost to the customer. The result was zero lost retail facings, and replacement products in the freezers within three weeks.

Had we not used Guardrails to guide our decision, we might have notified the customer that the problem was not our fault. They would have been forced to hire a food safety consulting firm to identify and resolve the problem, likely causing delays, and potentially leading to the loss of retail placements. Instead of engendering faith in our company and a positive outcome for all, we might well have lost our customer.

Another illustration: At one point at Ganeden, we had to decide whether or not to do business with a large potential customer. The customer came to us extremely excited about putting our probiotics into their kids' snack. Not just any snack, but one of the best-selling snacks in the country. The problem was the customer only wanted to put 10 percent of the required serving into each package of snacks, as that was the maximum cost they could afford while still maintaining their margins.

The account manager for the project produced every creative solution imaginable (salespeople are *very* creative when commissions are involved) to be able to work with this customer, but we simply couldn't allow them to use less than an efficacious amount of the probiotic. Plan B from the account manager was a massive price cut on the ingredient, which would cause a cascade effect with our other customers, who had agreements with provisions assuring best pricing.

Ultimately, we had to tell the account manager to communicate with his customer that we would simply not be able to meet their needs. In retrospect, the decision probably cost the salesperson more than $40,000 in commission and cost the business millions in revenue. But what it did do was allow us to stay within our Guardrails by moving us closer to the Destination (margin protection), and it was a Good decision in that consumers could remain assured that if our ingredient was in a product, the product would provide the desired clinical benefits. Hard decisions are hard, but if they are guided by solid

Guardrails, you can almost always look back and feel happy with the choices that were made.

Guardrailing as Road-Tripping

There are different versions of the way Guardrailing can simplify decision-making, given the great many individual, nuts-and-bolts choices a company must make along the way. Next, we'll expand our view to see how this method can be used as a decision-making model along your business's entire arc.

If you operate in the natural products industry—or if you simply had an especially good time in your youth—you have probably enjoyed your fair share of road trips. Those travels would have yielded adventures and, likely, entertaining misadventures that you have recounted to spit-takes and teasing around the campfire.

A well-executed road trip is a handy allegory for the successful trajectory of a business. What steps would you take to design a business the way you would plan a road trip? Not the twenty-year-olds-lost-in-the-desert kind of road trip, but the kind you would chart now, with your wits about you? What would you do to shape a path that leaves you full of soulful nourishment and actually gets you where you want to go?

Set Your Guardrails

Clearly define the Destination. Without a *clear* Destination, you wander aimlessly. As with a road trip in which identifying the Destination is essential to the journey, in business, an identified goal sets the course.

Tip: Lay out all of your potential options. Sell to a private equity firm, sell to a strategic, go public, run the business forever, etc. and determine which Destination best fits with your objectives and the objectives of your investors (if there are any)—that is, from a Destination *and* Goodness perspective.

Define the plan before you get started. A plan provides the details. Will you stop along the way to see the sights or head directly to the Destination? Where will you get fuel, and how will you pay for it? How long will the trip take? The plan is the roadmap, guiding day-to-day operations including vital decisions. So, in business terms:

Do you want to push for as quick a route as possible to your end goal, or are you interested in taking more time to cultivate Good along the way? How will you raise funds? From what sources, and via which human resources?

What's your ideal date for selling the company?

Tip: The plan is key—this is where you will decide if you need investment, what type of company structure you will have, manufacturing or not, how long the journey will be, etc. But don't worry, you're not alone—we will walk through this process in detail in the coming chapters. Until then, read on.

Determine who else will be in the car. Selecting good copilots in business is vital. Just as a road trip benefits from travelers with different personalities and skills (a mechanic, a navigator, someone focused, at least one person who is funny), the same holds true for your business team. Take a thorough, careful, unsentimental look at the people you have or are considering having as part of your leadership team. What roles are crucial to fill from the beginning? Who has the expertise for each role, and which positions are unfilled? And make sure you can imagine spending long, hardworking days with them. Do you have chemistry?

> Tip: Ensure that you are looking at the entire business life cycle as you plan for your team. Make sure the key bases are covered: CFO, COO, head of commercial, head of supply chain, operations staff, support, etc. Look beyond startup and into the distant future so you can plan accordingly. Clearly define what processes are required to keep your group of travelers on the right path.

Set the Destination. Plug your ultimate goal into your GPS, and ensure it uses the preferred route to take you to your Destination. Sometimes we are routed directly while other times what seems like a detour may be a well-informed path around traffic or construction—or worse yet—a washed out bridge. The key is to put processes in place that force you to review the Destination frequently and ensure that the course you are on will help you reach it.

Tip: From a business perspective, some examples may include assessments (which we will address in the coming pages), checking in with the team on a regular basis, and outside consumer surveys to gauge how well you are delivering on your commercial promise.

Assess and Adjust Your Guardrails

Set assessment parameters. You have been driving for three hours. Are you on course? Did the lunch stop at Subway turn you around and send you off in the wrong direction? Establish regular intervals to check your progress—the Destination is the key, but the journey can be unpredictable and course changes should be made intentionally. With your business, engage in assessments on a daily, weekly, monthly, quarterly, and annual basis.

Tip: Assessment tools are your friend here. Ensure that everything that matters to you and your business is able to be tracked and quantified. These assessment tools, for example an executive dashboard, should be simple to use and provide a complete picture of what is being monitored. The use of these simple tools can be the difference between heading directly to your Destination and veering off the road in unknown directions where it may be difficult to get back on track.

Determine Guardrail widths. A few other vehicles have joined your convoy and you've noticed that some of them keep bumping into the Guardrails or attempting to get off at unplanned exits.

Tip: As your team grows and your business becomes more complex you may add suppliers, partners and other resources that may not be as directed as you relating to Destination or processes, so you need to ensure you are able to adjust the width of the Guardrails to ensure you stay on the right path. An example may be bringing on a distributor that may have the best intentions but tends to work outside of the rules you've set for customer engagement. Due to their not working specifically within your Guardrails and if they are the only choice of supplier, you may need very narrow Guardrails to ensure they represent you well and move you toward your ultimate Destination.

Address how you will deal with obstacles. A boulder is blocking the road on a mountain overpass. Will you sit idly waiting for the highway service to come clear it or grab your tools (chisels, hammers, dynamite, whatever you packed for just such an occasion) and tackle it yourselves? Things happen—have a plan to address them calmly and rationally, and what may seem like a huge roadblock may simply be a minor stop along the path.

Tip: Some obstacles can be anticipated, and of course some can't, but it's essential that you devote time to researching the sorts of issues that may interfere with your progress. Meet with experts, put your heads together as a team, and develop a series of strategies for dealing with trouble as it arises.

Identify what will happen when you reach the Destination. Up ahead you see the lights of your journey's end. Are you ready? Arriving is a joyous occasion, one that is often also met with unexpected remorse and a desire to get back on the road and keep driving. You will think about how much you will miss your copilots and will have to face giving up the driver's seat. Keep in mind, the Destination is typically worth the trip.

Tip: As early as possible start to consider what will happen to the business, the offices, labs, people, everything when you reach your Destination. Having an idea as to what to expect when the Destination is reached is key so that expectations can be set from the very beginning. For example, don't sign a twenty-year lease when you know you will be selling the company in four years. That seems like a common sense suggestion, but these types of things happen and they often have an effect on value at exit.

Your Particular Company's Guardrails

The road trip analogy is meant to help you envision the general path your business will take, the challenges it will face, and the way Guardrailing can keep you aimed toward your Destination. It is a metaphor drawn to illustrate a methodology. Your actual route will have a unique combination of smooth stretches and bumpy interruptions, and it will require you to engage your capacity for flexibility from start to finish.

Keep your company's Destination and its commitment to Good in your sights as you move through this book. In the coming chapters, you will see Guardrailing applied to a series of situations you are likely to face, so you can make use of the approach in your business. Of course, not every scenario can be anticipated or covered in these pages, but my intention is to empower you with the fundamental capability to apply Guardrailing to any problem that arises so you can keep your company on track and rooted in its values.

Reflection Questions

Review a recent decision you or your company made that ended in a less than ideal outcome.

- Have you determined your Destination yet? If not— you will. If you have, start defining the Destination in detail.

- Were Guardrails used in making this decision?

- If they were used, were they too wide? Too narrow? Just right?

- What could have been done to ensure that the Guardrails were in place to provide a positive outcome?

- How will you handle these situations differently in the future?

- If Guardrails were not used, go ahead and replay the situation in your mind. How could you have set Guardrails that would have changed the outcome to something more positive?

CHAPTER 4

Start with Your Destination in Mind

It's not about the end. It's about the journey. Sometimes, the journey is way longer than you think. It's usually very different than you think it's going to be. If all you can focus on is the end goal—it's not going to be a very fun journey.

—KATE FLYNN, FOUNDER, SUN & SWELL

C lose, Kate, but without a Destination, a journey just goes on and on. You may arrive somewhere, but having a clear Destination makes the journey as fun as a journey like this can be. So, at the risk of some dead-horse beating, the first principle of Guardrailing is to start with your Destination in mind. However, determining that Destination can take a good deal of effort, arithmetic, and strategic thinking before you find your Destination's ultimate form: the glowing end goal of your company's leadership.

When I started my consulting engagement with Ganeden in 2006, I knew nothing about probiotics and what they could do. I learned that Ganeden, which was founded in 1997, was already distributing its supplements based on BC^{30} nationwide, but I knew little about microbiology and even less about food science and the other technologies the company was considering, such as waste remediation, soil management, and water treatment. So, I focused my attention on the markets Ganeden was already in, where they used probiotics to help support what I already did know plenty about: human and animal health.

With that focus in mind, I presented my findings to the founders, and we decided to move forward with a B2B ingredient business that focused on the many benefits of our amazing probiotic organism. While doing the early planning, I talked to the founders about their plans, and it was clear that selling the business was the primary focus. Although we had plenty of time to get there, considering that we were fundamentally beginning from nothing as an ingredient company, I wanted to get truly clear on the Destination. Picking an exit value of $100 million and market metrics of historical multiples of EBITDA (Earnings Before Interest, Taxes, Depreciation, and Amortization) of ten times, it seemed that we needed to build a business with roughly $10 million in EBITDA.

We then went through a variety of market-sizing exercises, where we looked at various products to determine what the revenue potential was on a per-customer basis. Doing that let us calculate how many customers we would need to reach our goal. But the math wasn't as easy as it sounded. One morning, as I was sitting down with our CEO, he said, "If we could just get BC[30] into every box of Cheerios sold, we could be well on our way to making this a wildly successful business." What a great idea! Until we calculated the servings sold each year by our friends at General Mills. As it turned out, we would not even be in the ballpark of our revenue dreams—not even if we snagged a global monopoly on probiotic Cheerios.

After that disappointing math, I went back to my office and calculated the margin we would need to produce adequate gross margin and EBITDA to help us reach our goals. I suggested a price that met our requirements—one that was approximately twice that of the next most expensive option in our space. But the numbers made sense, and I felt we should pin down the price and go to market as a super-premium ingredient.

On my recommendation, we set a price that provided the margins we needed, and then I sat down to look at potential acquirers for this yet-to-exist ingredient business. My initial list consisted of eight strategic buyers—each with a track record of doing acquisitions to grow or expand into new markets—and several private equity firms that were active in our space. We had our Destination established, and an array of potential purchasers who could make it real.

Were we putting the cart before the horse? Not one bit. We needed to know what we were aiming for before we took any other steps. Guardrail lesson in action: Identify your company's Destination first. Let everything else follow.

What Exactly Are You Selling?

Of course, setting a Destination like that assumes you have a clear image of what sort of company you will be creating. If you don't know that, you won't have a strong enough grasp of the journey you are embarking on. So, let's start with this critical bit of decision-making.

Over the course of my career, I have worked with individuals who wanted to go through the planning process with me—without actually knowing what they would be selling. It is hard—one might say impossible—to produce a great plan without first clearly defining your product.

Your first step is to determine precisely what you wish to sell. Is it a product? A service? An ingredient? A commodity that shoppers will find on the shelf of their local food co-op? Or is your concept in its infancy, a murky but energetically charged sense of an imagined item?

It can be rough to go from a seed of an idea to a highly refined image, and everyone starts with a lot of unknowns in their vision of what they will sell. You might try discussing what you want to produce in a letter to a trusted loved one—a letter you will never send. Or you might hole up in a hotel room for a weekend with your laptop and a stack of books and use your left brain to refine the nature of this product. You can even park yourself under a tree with a sketchbook and play visually with what it might be.

There are lots of ways to invite your creative self into the process of refining your concept. However you approach it, getting absolute clarity about what you are aiming to sell will get you on track, so you can define your Destination.

It may be obvious, but I'll say it again: During this conceptualizing phase, you want to consider the two key premises of Guardrailing (this is the easy part):

Destination: Does the product or service you want to take to market help you reach your Destination? (Well, I certainly hope so—Destinations aren't reached with simply hopes and dreams.

No, they require you to thoughtfully plan your Destination and then create something of value.)

Good(ness): Does the product or service cause any harm? If yes—well, do I even need to say it? If the answer to that first question is a no, then: Does the product or service create good in the world? If yes—get to work.

What *Not* to Do

Once you've defined the product, it is time to start building out the plan. And of course, if you're working toward success by Guardrailing, that plan must begin with its Destination.

But that's not how we've been taught to do it. That's just not how we've been taught to make plans.

Imagine that you started with the sort of traditional plan many of us have read about in business manuals or studied at university. Like the typical beginning company, you trusted that the list of actions you were given would offer a straightforward, linear plan to develop a "Friends and Family" pitch deck that would quickly secure an investment. Perhaps you found a free online template and set to work:

1. Executive Summary
2. Company and Business Description
3. Product and Services Line
4. Market Analysis
5. Marketing Plan
6. Sales Plan
7. Financial Plan

If you've been saturated in business "as usual," trained to pursue the establishment of a company using these supposedly tried and true methods, I suspect you are no stranger to this sort of list. As a newbie in the field, I had it memorized like a Bible passage.

Typically, a business in its launch phase addresses the market opportunity, determines its route to market, identifies how much money it will need and when it will need it, and sketches out an org chart. Working with that information, leadership creates a pitch deck in PowerPoint, and in a couple of months, they are confident in their process and ready to go. At that point, maybe they bring together family and friends for their first pitch, animated by the certainty that they'll blow their guests away.

Familiar?

A week or two later, the mystifying result: zero takers.

Maybe you've worked your way to this stage, or maybe you are at an earlier phase, still envisioning your plan. Either way, the path before you is clear. To avoid this heartbreak, you must begin with your Destination. Without the North Star of a clear, meaningful end goal, both your leadership team and anyone curious about funding or purchasing your company will be operating in a fog, unsure why or how they should support this project that means so much to you.

Start the Journey with the Destination

You've probably heard the Ralph Waldo Emerson quote, "It's not the Destination, it's the journey." This is often true—but if the Destination is the hospital emergency room, and you're going there to treat a broken arm, I do not think the journey is the most important thing to focus on. If midway through the journey to the ER, the driver saw a lovely sunset and decided to stop to enjoy the last glimpse of light, I am certain the patient would be less than happy. But that is the way many businesses operate. Diversions, pivots, and recalibration are the norm, and the Destination is a garbled bunch of options that all seem equally enticing.

To take the road trip parallel a bit further, imagine pooling resources with your buddies, all of you bursting with energy and weary of stagnation, jumping in the car, and speeding free of your boring town. Now, you're on the highway. Everyone's got a different idea about where to go. You're hemorrhaging cash on gas, getting lost on side roads, finding yourselves in pointless arguments, and all the while no one is leading the way to a glorious end point.

All that human and monetary capital is being squandered, when you could have headed straight for the rainbow mists of Big Sur or the stunning red arches of Moab and be stretching your legs right this minute.

If you'd only determined your Destination first.

For a business owner, CEO, or executive team, the Destination needs to be key. A well-planned journey should get everyone to the Destination on time and with fuel left in the tank. Your investors, clients, partners, team, and the people in your personal life will all greatly appreciate this focus. Because it is so integral to successful Guardrailing, let's look at Destination-first planning in detail.

And a word about the tone of this chapter: we're about to shift gears from traveling metaphors at this point to zero in on your needs using business speak, because the precise language is necessary. And if you're launching a company, you are probably bilingual in *businessese* anyhow!

How to Determine Your Destination

Whether you are a startup or an established company looking to improve your focus on value generation, gather your leadership team and give serious attention to the following questions.

- *Why* are you building the business?
- *For whom* are you building the business?

Fortunately, the potential answers are limited and can be decided on by asking:

What will we do with this business in the long term?

The most obvious options are:

1. Create a sustainable business to hand down to family.
2. Go public and run it as a public enterprise.
3. Sell it to a strategic (i.e., a company in the same space that is doing, or wants to do, what your business is doing.)
4. Sell it to a private equity firm.

There are other options, but these are the four most common end goals, and there are pros and cons for each. Running a business to be passed on to a successor or focusing on a future public offering are specific options, and whole libraries worth of volumes have been written about these two options. Therefore, as noted earlier, this book focuses on selling the business you've built, and the strategies and insights that fill the rest of this book are designed to help you reach that Destination.

Getting Specific About Selling

When we look at the options for selling, there is an exercise that all entrepreneurs should undertake: identifying the future buyers, up front and in detail.

By assembling a list of potential acquirers and understanding the value drivers for each, you can gather insights into what can create enterprise value that will maximize the price paid by the ultimate buyer. Identifying potential buyers also allows you to keep the focus on the potential buyers' interests while remaining focused on the Destination.

Whether your company is a B2B or B2C, you will want to review the universe of buyers—specifically strategics and PE firms—by doing the following:

- Research who competes in your company's space directly and identify the ones that participate in the market without a directly competitive product.

- Develop a list of 5–10 buyers who are focusing on solutions in the company's space.

- Determine which companies have a history of acquiring companies that are a strategic fit with their business.

- Once these potential acquirers are identified, look at their previous acquisitions to determine the typical multiples paid for similar companies.

This analysis should provide an estimate as to what it will take for your business to create the exit value that will attract the type of purchasing company you desire. For example, if an acquirer—either strategic or PE—has historically paid a multiple equal to ten times EBITDA, and the founders want to sell the business for $50 million, they will need to generate EBITDA of $5 million. So, when approaching that milestone, the team may begin considering initiating a process to sell the business.

On the other hand, the team may decide to continue to grow the business, and they may adjust their Guardrails as they relate to their exit value, but they will continue to have clear direction toward the ultimate Destination. Of course, there are many other factors that affect the value of a business—but when starting off on a journey, it is enough to define the buyer universe and exit target value. There will be plenty of time to adjust the Guardrails as the journey continues.

Considerations Specific to Private Equity Buyers

To get more "granular," as folks these days like to say, the process with private equity buyers is similar, but there are other options that are typically not available when selling to a strategic. PE firms often want the management team to remain with the business and retain partial ownership, which aligns the management team's incentives with those of the PE firm.

For instance, a PE firm may acquire 75 percent of a business, leaving the remaining 25 percent in the hands of the businesses' management team. This allows the management team to have an initial liquidity event, while also benefiting from the resources provided by the PE firm to expedite growth and plan an exit—often to a strategic buyer, in five years or so.

This approach presents a potential win-win scenario for the business, but it may require a commitment from the management team to stay through another phase of growth before securing their second, often more substantial, liquidity event when the PE firm decides to exit. This contrasts with a business sold to a strategic buyer, where there is often an opportunity for the founders to transition out of the business to focus on other pursuits.

Still with me?

Creating a Destination-First Business Plan

Remember that numbered business plan we talked about earlier in this chapter? If your company is launching itself with a to-do list that follows those traditional business rules, then your company is not starting with its end goal in mind. This means that you have not answered two fundamental questions that would guide you: Why are you building the business? And for whom?

What would happen if your company developed its plan using the Guardrail approach, with Destination-focused planning as its organizing principle? You could embark on a journey to grow your company with your Destination—selling—as your guiding aim. Thanks to that focus, when you arrived at the stage of your initial investor pitch session, your team could communicate confidence about this chosen Destination, remembering that it isn't absurd to sell to a strategic or PE firm—it's logical. At the investor presentation, your audience would have a precise direction to keep in mind in evaluating their potential investment. Attendees could then consider key issues with clarity:

- The timeframe for holding the investment.

- Risks that might arise relating to future dilution (the reduction in the percentage of existing shareholders' ownership in a company when it issues new shares of stock)

- The need for additional capital to grow the business to the point where it would be attractive to an ultimate acquirer.

A robust Q&A session might challenge your presenters about the specifics of reaching the proposed Destination. However, since your team knows where the company is headed, even with a number of what-if questions, they should be able to provide information that helps direct the company toward your Destination every time. Consider your emerging business in such a gathering: If you put in the time to clarify your Destination, you prepare your team to handle unforeseen challenges. Your work setting Guardrails and establishing your end goal can give you the capacity to answer tough questions and persuade skeptics from the start.

Not only does Destination-first planning set your company up for success in the immediate term, but the same Guardrails that you established early on can also prove key to future decision-making and keep your business on the right path. Of course, that path will not be straight or predictable. As with a road trip, your company GPS will maintain the Destination as the target, but there will be occasions where rerouting is required. All the same, by beginning with your end goal in mind, you can watch your project progress and your Destination get clearer and closer with each passing day.

Reflection Questions

For these reflections, I encourage you to gather your leadership team, along with any mentors who shine a light on your blind spots, and do some brainstorming together.

Determine your company's Destination:

- How much will you sell your company for?
- What is the time frame to do so?
- What is the revenue/EBITDA needed to justify your sale price?
- What are five strategic and five private equity firms that could potentially acquire the business when you reach your Destination?

CHAPTER 5

Create Your Business Roadmap

*First and foremost, any brand or business
should be born from passion and purpose.*

—GT Dave, Founder, CEO/CMO, GT's Living Foods

Destination-first planning will save you headaches, protect you from financial aches, and potentially let you prevent avoidable catastrophes. So, once you've set your Destination, your next step is to define your company's journey in detail by creating a map with that specific Destination in mind.

Developing a Map

Remember the traditional business plan presented in chapter 4? Well, here it is again—except this time, it's been edited so that Guardrailing places the Destination at the top of the list. In the descriptions below, you'll discover my suggestions about the timing of when you might address each item in your actual journey, but for planning's sake, this order is appropriate. The components of a typical business plan aren't wrong; they're just generally approached out of order. Guardrailing teaches us that if we begin with the Destination, we can assemble a list of necessary elements to focus on while always keeping our end goal in view.

1. Identify Destination
2. Company & Business Description
3. Product & Services Line
4. Market Analysis
5. Marketing Plan
6. Sales Plan
7. Financial Plan
8. Executive Summary

If you look carefully, though, you'll notice that this new business plan doesn't just add "Identify Destination" as the first step—it also moves the former first step, the executive summary, all the way to the end. After all, you can't summarize what you're all about until you actually *know* what you're all about.

In the next few pages, you'll find an overview of a standard business plan, with the actions you'll need to take to advance the progress of your company toward its end goal. Pay special attention to the comments in italics, where I've presented the Guardrailing techniques that are likely to best help your business launch, thrive, and become ready for sale. If you follow the Guardrailing guidance closely and carefully, you'll be on your way to having a solid map for your company's journey.

1. Destination

This first one is simple. At the risk of sounding like a broken record, I truly can't emphasize this core principle of Guardrailing enough: *A business that is set up to succeed envisions its Destination first and follows with a detailed plan to get there.*

2. Company and Business Description

If you know without a doubt that your product is a Consumer Packaged Good, great. Feel confident choosing a Business-to-Consumer or Direct-to-Consumer model. But I cannot tell you how many times I have seen startups begin with what they are sure is a CPG product, only to ultimately sell into the Business-to-Business space.

When you define your Destination, you may realize that the team lacks the skills needed to focus on consumer products, and if you move forward with a CPG product, the company will face undue financial strain. Having this important realization early could save your company hundreds of thousands if not millions of dollars! Often, companies spin their wheels for years before recognizing that the process of creating and selling a finished product is better suited to companies that specialize in consumer brands. *As you draft your plan, give thorough consideration to the risks and benefits of each possible route.*

3. Product and Services

A critical decision in navigating product and service offerings is the choice between manufacturing the ingredient in-house or leveraging the capabilities of a Contract Manufacturing Organization (CMO). It often surprises me how many companies intend to produce their own materials. Some may have produced small amounts of an ingredient or product in a small-scale setting, but achieving scalability can be an intricate ordeal, fraught with obstacles—especially when driven by control issues or ego-centric motives.

This question prompts a fundamental build vs. buy analysis, guided by the principles of Guardrails. Key questions to address include:

- **Manufacturer Availability.** *Are there manufacturers available to produce the product to your required quality standards?*

- **Production Capacity.** *Do the manufacturers have capacity to meet your needs now and as you approach your Destination?*

If these needs are all met, then outsource and keep your business asset light and nimble, while ensuring you have an outstanding relationship with your CMO. If capacity is not available, or if the technology to manufacture your product does not exist— make very, very certain that the economics of your business work and that the demand exists to produce a positive ROI on your manufacturing assets.

4. Market Analysis

Your business—actually, any business—must perform a thorough analysis of the market, assessment of opportunities, and product overview. This allows your team to watch the Guardrails while observing the market so your company can be assured that its product is novel, needed, and of impeccable quality. And when I say watch the Guardrails, I really mean watch the market. From Google alerts and market reports to participation in trade associations and networking with industry thought leaders, you *cannot* know too much about your market. Missing a big market move or news and being left behind is inexcusable in this day and age, given the massive amount of data that is available. With deep market perspectives, you can identify opportunities and begin to identify potential customers, by name, who would benefit from the product.

This process is incredibly important and is especially relevant in the natural products space where passion occasionally makes us oblivious to market realities and optimistically sticking with opinions after they have been disproven is common in passion/mission-based businesses.

I recall walking the floor of the Fancy Food show one year when it seemed like every other booth was introducing a new salsa. I asked one of the multitudes of salsa companies what made their product stand out from the pack, and their answer was sincere but all too common: "This is my grandmother's recipe and everyone who has ever tasted it tells me that it is the best they have ever had—so I quit my job, mortgaged my house, and am all in." I'm betting grandma would have used some good ol' grandma logic and suggested that her family stick with their day jobs and keep enjoying the spicy Mexican deliciousness at family gatherings, or make it and sell it at local farmers' markets.

A basic market analysis, guided by Guardrails, would have shown the entrepreneur that grandma was right—the market was satisfied with the current offerings, and in fact oversaturated. That simple analysis would have likely saved all those soon-to-be-defunct salsa companies much time and money.

Through the use of Guardrails, an entrepreneur can look at their ideas objectively, by gathering data that supports their decision to make the journey in the first place. With Guardrails in place, a Destination may be identified. But when determining the market value of the opportunity, those same Guardrails may inform the entrepreneur that the Destination is simply too crowded to meet the financial return requirements, and the Destination should be reevaluated or reset altogether.

5. Marketing Plan

Marketing. I could draft an entire book on marketing—many people have, and many more will in the future. But how does Guardrailing apply to marketing? Isn't marketing a creative endeavor that needs to be unconstrained, so ideas like Nike's "Just Do It" can flow freely from brilliant minds?

Somewhat, but not really. At the risk of oversimplifying, new companies need to market *themselves* (i.e., the company and its story) before they market the items they will offer. Early marketing brings attention to unknowns with potential, so people know that they exist, what they are doing, and how they are going to make a difference. Once that foundation has been laid, the focus should shift from promoting the company to promoting the company's products. Over time, the company, its founders, and its story will become less important value drivers. As that is happening, the company should undergo a shift to focus on the product or service, as that is what will ultimately be sold when the company is acquired.

Think about a real-world example: When a company like Ganeden sells, the acquirer will typically not put marketing dollars behind the "Ganeden" brand. Instead, the acquirer puts their money behind what they purchased—in Ganeden's case, our organism BC[30] and its related IP. *When Guardrails are set around marketing initiatives, the Guardrails start wide and become quite narrow as the company evolves.* By the time the company is mature and running smoothly, there should be a very ROI-focused marketing approach—one geared toward selling more of your products, not winning awards or having your company name emblazoned on every T-shirt at the latest Expo.

6. Sales Plan

Once you've finally addressed all of those huge questions, *you'll need to consider the route to market*. After all, you will have to sell your product *somehow*. Many companies believe in the "build it and they will come" approach—which in nearly every instance I've encountered has been an abysmal failure. Luckily, Guardrails and a strong focus on your Destination can keep your business from doing the same.

To succeed, your marketing program must identify how to reach out to potential clients in your market and focus on generating qualified leads. But those leads aren't going to close themselves, and the founders can only sell for so long before the business requires a go-to-market team. This team can be a distribution partner or direct sales team, but either way, the decision should be guided by Guardrails set wide enough for you to try a few different routes to market before settling in on a strategy. Often, different sales approaches are required domestically and internationally, and there are ways to integrate referral partners, distributors, and a dedicated sales team to create a hybrid team consisting of direct employees and external partners. Guardrails can be set at different widths depending upon the maturity of the program.

As an example, when we first started selling BC^{30} at Ganeden, we had a single part-time account manager (the other part of his job was setting up internal processes), so we augmented his responsibilities with a dedicated distributor. We worked with that distributor until we had revenue and a pipeline that justified hiring additional internal team members, and ultimately, we left the distributor and took all domestic sales activities in-house. But keep in mind that distributors know the market and are typically well known—so treat them well and ensure they have a tail (i.e., are paid past the end of their engagement for the accounts they brought in) for a year or two. Remember, they got you to where you are, and you may need them again in the future. Plus—it's a Good thing to do. Especially as you enter into new international markets—the distributor can typically help with registrations and regulatory work and should be rewarded for their contributions.

7. Financial Plan

As you no doubt know, you need a financial plan. And more than that, you need a good, defensible financial plan that can pass muster with financial professionals. Perhaps you're already at work on one. As you consider this aspect of mapping your business, remember that Guardrails should guide every aspect of your plan, from start to finish. *Financial Guardrails are placed narrowly to ensure compliance with laws and standards.* Why? Because there are laws, standards, and regulations to follow—and not following them can have extremely negative legal and financial consequences. And of course, you have to adhere to those laws and regulations on top of the expectations of your board, team, and investors.

So, when it comes to financial planning and reporting, don't try to reinvent the wheel. Financial reporting, primarily through a P&L, balance sheet, and cash flow statement, is very standard, and reporting to standards will keep everyone in the loop without them having to decipher your unique (a.k.a. poor) way of reporting financials.

Enough said about that for now, though—there is plenty more on financing in the upcoming chapter on fundraising.

8. Executive Summary

Traditionally, business plans often tell you to write the executive summary first thing. In contrast, I always recommend writing this section at the end of the process, after the details of the rest of the plan have been established. After all, developing a meandering, overly optimistic elevator pitch without hammering out the specifics of the journey to your Destination leads to confusion—or worse, a lack of confidence in company leadership.

Additionally, many people get stuck at this step, spending far too much time and money crafting catchy mission and vision statements. While these elements are certainly important, a clear, honest declaration of mission and vision are sufficient to start, and they can always be honed down the road.

Guardrailing as an Adaptable Practice

It's important to keep in mind that Guardrailing is an approach a business can use for just about any decision—large or small. We have already discussed some of the major crossroads a company might face and the ways Guardrailing can be used to tackle those moments of decision-making. But throughout your journey from inception to sale, you will be faced with myriad unanticipated dilemmas that require unexpected decisions. So, as you integrate Guardrailing into your business and processes, view it as a practice—a method of inquiry that allows you to cut through all levels of difficulties while keeping a steady view of your Destination and your commitment to Good as you move forward.

Here is an example from my days with Ganeden. Things were going great at the company, and we were growing at a very respectable clip. Then, without warning, the sole source supplier of our key ingredient informed us that they would be unable to ship the ingredient for several months. We had a track record of never missing shipping dates and never disappointing a customer, but suddenly we were faced with not having access to the inventory that our customers needed to meet their production schedules.

We had Guardrails in place relating to inventory and how we handled last-minute shipping requests, but we didn't have a plan for a disaster like this. So, time to create new Guardrails for guidance.

We could have handled this crisis by contacting our customers to let them know that, for reasons beyond our control, we would not be able to ship the material, and therefore they would not be able to produce the products that contained our ingredient. But that did not seem like a particularly good option. We could have also relegated the inventory we did have to our top customers—but all of our customers, whether buying one kilo or ten thousand, were equally important, and so once again, the Guardrails wouldn't allow that option to even be considered.

Ultimately, what we did was rally the team and call all of our customers who had purchased in the prior months to ask them if they had any excess inventory on hand. Much to our surprise (and delight), many of our customers did have inventories on hand, ranging from small offerings to enormous quantities. Once we'd established that there was a source of ingredient we could tap, we made a new deal with our customers: We agreed to pay for the shipping and replacement of their ingredient, if they allowed us to take some of the material that they would not need in the upcoming quarter so that we could support our other customers. Without exception, our customers stepped up and helped us, and we missed zero shipment deadlines, keeping production on schedule for all of our clients.

Of course, our entire team aged ten years over the course of those events. However, by producing a creative solution that was enabled by the strong relationships we had with our customers and partners, we were nevertheless able to get through that challenge without abandoning our commitment to our values or losing sight of our Destination.

When something like that happens, it's the job of the company to come up with a plan B, plan C, and sometimes a plan D to make sure that if the same thing happens in the future, Guardrails and contingency plans are already in place. That is how you ensure that a short-term problem does not turn into a long-term catastrophe for the business.

As for Ganeden's new Guardrails, at the end of the day, we and our supplier were forced to develop new contingency plans. Specifically, our Guardrails indicated that we needed to hold more bulk inventory and locate a backup supplier in case a similar situation ever occurred in the future.

Guardrailing Works Even Better at the Top

I once was an executive at a company that sold and provided services around automated defibrillators (AEDs) that were installed in corporate offices and other places where people gathered. When I arrived at the company, they were the distributor for a single manufacturer, and planned their services around that manufacturer's specific device. The goal of the organization (and its investors), through the lens of Guardrailing, was to sell the business in the coming year or two—but providing services and equipment for a single manufacturer would obviously limit options when it came time to exit the business. (Some of you may be saying, "Yeah, no kidding," but as you will see in your own businesses, not looking at the Destination up front can get you into these situations, and sometimes it is hard if not impossible to change course once you have set sail.) Therefore, we decided to reach out to all manufacturers of these medical devices and offer the same solution for their devices as well.

This wasn't a popular decision in some parts of the business as many of the employees of the company had become quite enmeshed in the culture of that single manufacturer, but the executive team saw the benefits of using the Guardrailing process to evaluate its decisions around exit options and endorsed the plan wholeheartedly. And they were right to do so: every manufacturer that we contacted agreed to work with us, and it expanded our market by five times.

At the end of the day, we had access to and used all of the various mainstream AEDs and were able to provide services around them. When it came time to begin exploring options to exit the business, we were no longer limited to a narrow universe of buyers—instead, we had opened up our options to include selling the business to any of the manufacturers we were working with, as well as similar service providers. We approached each of the manufacturers we were working with and told them that we would be selling the business, and that we would most likely be selling it to an AED manufacturer. Without our actually saying it, that option led the other manufactures to believe that they would lose the ability to offer that service—after all, they certainly wouldn't be welcome to provide service on their competitors' devices.

So, at the end of the day, we sold the company to one of the larger, publicly traded manufacturers of automated defibrillators, and they became the only AED manufacturer to offer the ancillary services that our company had become known for. The services that we were offering to all of the large manufacturers of the medical devices were then exclusively offered by the company that acquired the business, creating a competitive advantage for them and leaving the other manufacturers looking for a solution to a problem they hadn't anticipated. For the acquiring company, in addition to the competitive advantage, the ownership of (what was previously our) service company also represented a sales opportunity, as they were able to go into the market and replace some of the competitive devices with their own so that our previous clients could continue to receive the same services as before. Guardrailing applied when we decided to widen the Guardrails to allow us to expand beyond our initial manufacturer—and Guardrailing succeeded when we sold the company for twice what we had set as the lowest acceptable price.

All this is to say that while Guardrailing works across the board, the higher up in an organization this model can be used, the simpler the process of adoption and the higher the chances of long-term success. The team at that AED company that was comfortable working with the single manufacturer's device was happy with things the way they were—but Guardrails helped inform them of the fact that their original plans were limiting their opportunities and hurting their ability to reach their Destination.

Let Luck Happen

In business, serendipitous moments often play a pivotal role. Luck, that unforeseen element, can be the catalyst that propels a venture to success. While meticulous planning and strategic decision-making are essential, unexpected encounters can shape the path of a business. When you capitalize on the kismet of connecting with those further along the path, you may find your business propelling itself forward. A carefully drafted plan, a map for your journey, is crucial. But not all opportunities are things you can plan for. As you progress, don't be afraid to scan the horizon for unexpected sparkles of luck. After all, what's the fun of creating a business if you aren't keeping an eye out for the sparkles?

Reflection Questions

Using the Guardrail guidance in this chapter, take some time with your team to shape an optimal business plan. Whether you don't yet have a plan for your company or you've already drafted a business plan, look back at the highlighted strategies throughout this chapter to make sure that you're on track.

- What adjustments can you make to map your journey while keeping your Destination as your North Star?

- Have you considered the Goodness of the steps in the journey and the overall Goodness of the business in general?

- How can you refine or develop aspects of your plan that feel underexplored?

CHAPTER 6

Fundraising

Fundraising is very much selling vision and storytelling and focusing on how your market evolves over time or changes because of the product or the service that you built or introduced.

—Yaw Aning, Co-founder and CEO of Malomo

If you applied the Guardrailing concepts in the previous chapter to your company's business plan, it's very likely that your questions created more questions, and that big concepts yielded specific concerns for you and your leadership team to address. Maybe your growing to-do list looks like some variation on this:

- Set up IT systems
- Review office lease
- Find a benefit plan
- Find a 401k provider
- Evaluate permanent vs. shared lab space
- Create equipment list and budget
- Build out staffing needs
- Generate HR handbook

- Assemble investor list and begin outreach

- Determine trade associations to join

- Research trade shows to attend

- Find a coffee service (especially important) (!) (!!)

Overwhelmed? You're in luck, because at this point, only two words on that list matter: *investor* and *outreach*. The rest of your plans don't mean a whole lot without money. Another way to say it is that without proper funding, your Destination is nothing more than an idea.

All the to-do lists and action plans in the world will not help an undercapitalized business. At this point, your job is to get to work assembling an investor list and developing resources. You may well have read your share of fundraising books, but important nuances are ignored in typical "Raising Capital for My Business" manuals. Often, these volumes neglect to urge readers to forecast pre-revenue, revenue growth to break-even, growth after profitability, and exit target planning.

When you begin to develop the model on which your funding plan will be based, develop specific Guardrails to assure that you remain on course to your Destination. I'm not going to get into the minutia relating to fundraising, though I encourage those of you who are now or soon will be raising money to do your homework. Read more (see www.GrowthWays.com/resources), talk to experts, and explore your options *before* you start talking to potential bankers or investors—it will save you a great deal of time (and possible embarrassment). There are basics that you must consider regardless of funding options, and below are some areas you must incorporate into your financial calculus as you create a fundraising strategy. Key here is ensuring that you consider Guardrails for each area so that you are able to adjust the plan as needed.

- **Startup costs.** Include all one-time expenses associated with setting up the business, such as legal fees, registration costs, lease deposits, equipment purchases, initial inventory, branding, and marketing expenses.

- **Operating expenses.** Factor in the ongoing costs required to run the business, including rent, utilities, insurance, salaries, raw materials, packaging, shipping, and any other recurring expenses.

- **Technology and software.** Utilize the best available (and most affordable) technologies to limit manual tasks. Include costs for necessary software, laboratory tools, and technology infrastructure, such as inventory management and enterprise, resources planning (ERP) systems, customer relationship management (CRM) software, various cloud services, and the development and upkeep of your web presence.

- **Research and development (R&D).** If your company is a science-based company, there will be initial and ongoing R&D and clinical expenses that must be accounted for. Get outside advice on how expensive the clinical data you need will be. Then, plan on spreading your R&D spend over the entire life of the company, so you can continuously improve the clinical support of products and generate the greatest amount of value in the long term.

- **Regulatory and compliance costs.** Include predicted costs associated with obtaining necessary certifications, approvals, and compliance with relevant regulations. Don't forget international costs if you plan on selling beyond your home country—the more places you can legally sell your product, the greater the value when you reach your Destination.

- **Marketing and advertising.** Budget for marketing campaigns, promotional activities, trade show participation, and advertising efforts to create brand awareness and attract customers.

- **Sales and distribution.** Consider expenses related to sales efforts, such as team salaries, commissions, and distribution costs. Keep in mind that you will need plenty of face-to-face time with customers to become the next "big thing," so add plenty of (frugal) travel to the sales budget.

- **Contingency fund.** Not knowing how long the initial regulatory, clinical, and revenue generation periods might take, set aside a portion of capital as a contingency fund to address unexpected expenses or unforeseen challenges that may arise during the initial phase of your business.

- **Working capital.** It is imperative to ensure for adequate levels of working capital to cover day-to-day expenses and maintain sufficient inventory levels to bridge the gap between paying vendors and payment by clients.

- **Debt servicing.** Even if you don't think you will need it, there may come a day when you need debt financing to support your activities, so be sure to include this.

- **Tax provisions.** Count on early losses. In other words, early tax ramifications will be insignificant to cash, but in the later stages of the business, you will use up all the carried forward losses and you'll be paying taxes on your handsome profits.

- **Timeline considerations.** Do not raise more money than is needed (plus contingency), as the money is far more expensive early on when the valuation is low. If the stars align and you execute on your plan, you may find that this initial raise is the only equity financing you will need to do—thereby protecting all shareholders from dilution. Proper timing and types of financing can be a significant factor when you reach your Destination, as you don't want to take in more cash than you'll need (which would result in early dilution), and you certainly don't want to get short on cash in the middle of getting started.

- **Cash flow analysis.** Finally, once a finance number is settled on, you need to run detailed cash flow analysis with a variety of "what-if" scenarios. That way, you can make sure that the business will have sufficient cash on hand to cover expenses and maintain a healthy financial position. You may need to adjust your anticipated total based on these considerations.

At the end of this incredibly arduous exercise, you should have a number that will get the company up and running to the point where you are producing recurring and predictable revenue. As always, under-promise and over-deliver on your plan. That way, future rounds, if needed, will go more smoothly than if you had missed the numbers in your original plan.

Keep Your Guardrails Flexible

Regardless of the time you put into your funding plan, chances are your end funding projection will need to be revised more than once. It's essential to approach these adjustments with flexibility and a focus on aligning strategies with your company's overall mission. Which is another way of saying you'll need to rely on the flexibility of your Guardrails, keeping your eye on those two key principles: your company's relationship to Good and its ultimate Destination.

One company I consulted for needed to reduce its funding goal, as they were having trouble closing investors because some of the spending seemed excessive, especially early on. But no one on the team wanted to budge and let go of "their" needs. After reviewing their numbers, I saw a straightforward way to reduce their cash needs by $500,000, possibly more. But it would require compromise by their head of science.

Initially, she balked at giving up her dream lab to rent a shared lab space. I explained that I had other clients who used them, that they were popping up everywhere, and that they regularly offered small companies better equipment than they could typically afford. After the science head realized a shared lab wouldn't jeopardize the firm's strong science Guardrail of producing high-quality data internally and on short time frames, she agreed. The head of science also made sure the team agreed that down the road, they would look at building out their own lab should they outgrow the capacity of their shared space. Ultimately, the company went with the shared lab space—and the company never even needed the dedicated lab. Therefore, when they sold the company, the acquiring company was able to focus on continuity of service rather than determining what to do with a redundant R&D facility. The moral of this story: When faced with funding challenges, consider creative solutions and compromises that align with your Destination.

Cautionary Tales

It's worth looking at how errors can be made in this arena of fundraising, since mistakes are great teachers. And Lord knows I've seen—and made—my fair share of fundraising mistakes. Here are a couple of juicy ones.

Raising money for a company is never fun, and at the end of the day, battle wounds will be worn by everyone involved. I was once advising a company that was preparing to raise money to expand operations, with an eye on selling the company a few years later. Sitting in on the pitch, I listened to the founder (chair) and his son (president and CEO) discuss all aspects of the business, ranging from their sales pipeline and production schedule to their long-term goals and timing on an exit. Never once did the father-son team ever mention their management team or who did the work at the company. They didn't even mention the management team's names or qualifications in the

CIM (Confidential Information Memorandum) or management presentation.

When a question was finally asked about the company's staff, the duo mentioned that they had complete control of the company and knew everything that was going on with customers, production, etc. They acknowledged that they did have a good team, but no one on the team was irreplaceable, and beyond that, the systems they had in place allowed the company to virtually run itself.

However, the use of proceeds as illustrated in the pitch deck showed that they needed to make some key hires to grow and shore up their technical team. The potential investors tried to identify the members of the team, but the chair only presented an organization chart with titles and no names. When asked about this, the father mentioned that they had tried to work with a VC firm previously, and that they believed the VC firm had tried to poach their employees, so they would not be "sharing" the names of the individuals in the various roles. You'll be shocked to learn that the potential investor(s) decided against "sharing" cash with the mystery team led by this paranoid duo.

Another example of fundraising gone bad was when a company brought in an investor with extremely onerous terms. So onerous that when they went to sell the business, that investor had such over-the-top rights that they could have potentially stopped the transaction. This would have cost the other investors, who had much more in terms of capital invested, hundreds of millions of dollars. The company had done their fundraising too late, which meant they were almost out of cash and were desperate for an investor.

This type of situation typically scares off the better investors and leaves the investment to firms that are the corporate financial world's version of loan sharks. They have a "take the money or go broke" attitude, and in this instance, that was the only option. So, the company took the money, only to find that when they went to sell the company—at a lower valuation than the last round of financing—the only investor that was made whole was that final investor. This last one in the pool made over seven times their money, while everyone else lost most of their initial investment, and the founders and employees received next to nothing.

This company knew it would need more capital well before they needed it—over two years earlier—but they kicked the can down the street, hoping for a revenue windfall that never happened. If they had used their Guardrails and raised cash ahead of their needs, they would have stayed on the path to their Destination and exited the business with a host of happy stakeholders. But instead, they waited too long to raise cash and wound up taking an investment that ultimately hurt the company and its stakeholders.

Establishing a Board of Advisors

As your business matures, it is well worth your while to look at assembling a group of advisors. You'll need to know more than you currently do, and if you haven't done it yet, now is the time to bring together a circle of experts to provide you and your team with guidance.

I can't stress enough the need for quality advisors. Whether you go with an informal board of advisors, a formal board of directors, or specialized scientific advisors, it is incredibly important to have counselors who have "been there and done that." It is also important that your team of entrepreneurs understand that not every bit of advice the advisors give is going to be in full alignment with those of the company.

While it seems like a clever idea to have a group of advisors who agree wholeheartedly with the management team, disagreements often produce the best outcomes. The management team may become myopic and disregard the guidance of advisors who do not agree with them, or they may have experience that contradicts the plans or ideas of the team. In such cases, it is crucial to look at the contradictory advice as coming from a place of concern and experience. All too often the management team fears being found out as not knowing everything about their business, market, etc., and so they go shopping around for advisors who agree with them blindly. Boards loaded with allies of the CEO will likely make decisions that appease the egos of the management team—but may well not provide guidance that is in the best interest of the company and its stakeholders.

My advice? Management teams should learn to listen, evaluate, and take advice. It isn't easy, and it makes for the occasional prickly board or advisory meeting, but the company will be better for it.

Finding Your Number

Getting ready to ask for millions of dollars is often daunting to newbie entrepreneurs. Impostor syndrome can take hold along with general doubts. But while raising $5 million might feel like climbing Mount Everest for new (and many not so new) entrepreneurs, many investors and bankers treat it like a stroll to basecamp. Raising funds is hard. But there is a massive amount of money out there looking for the right investment. If you want to produce what investors are looking for, it is time for your team to get to work assembling the dreaded CIM (Confidential Information Memorandum).

CIM Basics

A CIM is a commonly used document that includes all the standard information found in an initial investment pitch deck, but tells a far more detailed and sophisticated story, one presented to "real money people."

It is important to understand the value of using language that the audience understands and respects. A pitch deck aimed toward friends and family investors is typically focused on points that resonate with them, seem like strong ideas, and convey the passion and excitement of the entrepreneurs. On the other hand, a CIM typically follows a format familiar to sophisticated investors. The data is presented in a way that tells the story of the business, explains the opportunity, and describes the plan from start to finish in a way that allows the investors to determine whether a particular investment fits with their business model.

The CIM is often prepared by an investment banker that you have enrolled to help with your fundraise. But with smaller raises, it is often hard—if not impossible—to find any bankers willing to take the project. So, if you're in that boat, then now is the time where you become your own banker by creating your CIM. Doing so has a couple different benefits. First off, you save your business massive fees. And second, who is more qualified to talk about a business than those who founded it? So, let's jump into the basics of this complex but important document.

A typical CIM often includes the following key points:

- **Executive summary.** A brief overview of the company and its mission, product or service, market opportunity, and the amount of capital you are seeking. (As with other materials, when you're drafting your CIM, write the summary last.)

- **Company overview.** A detailed description of the company's background, history, and legal structure, with mention of key milestones achieved to date.

- **Market opportunity.** The target market and the problem your product or service aims to solve. Market size, growth trends, and potential for disruption are included. Note: Investors love talking about the TAM (Total Addressable Market)—even if TAM numbers are usually based on informed dart tosses.

- **Product or service description.** A comprehensive overview of the product or service, its features, and how it works, along with its development status and any unique features.

- **Value proposition.** The unique attributes and benefits of your product or service, and how it addresses the needs of the target market better than existing solutions.

- **Business model.** An outline of how the company plans to generate revenue and achieve profitability, produce their product, and maintain a competitive advantage throughout the life of the business.

- **Competitive landscape.** An identification of direct and indirect competitors, their strengths and weaknesses, and a highlighting of your competitive advantages.

- **Go-to-market strategy.** The marketing and sales approach your company will use to reach your target audience effectively, including pricing and margin considerations, and a discussion of any partnerships or distribution agreements.

- **Financial projections.** Detailed financial forecasts, including income statements, balance sheets, and cash flow projections for at least the next three years. Assumptions and key drivers should be included.

- **Use of funds.** A clear statement of how the capital will be utilized, including specific allocation of funds for various activities (e.g., product development, marketing, hiring).

- **Management team.** An introduction to the key members of the management team, their expertise, and their relevant experience. Any advisors or mentors should be included here.

- **Intellectual property.** If applicable, information on patents, trademarks, copyrights, or other intellectual property rights owned by the company. It is also important to highlight how the company will protect and expand its IP over time.

- **Risks and mitigations.** It shows a depth of thought when a business identifies potential risks and challenges the company may face and an explanation of the strategies in place to mitigate them.

- **Exit strategy.** Potential exit options for investors, with a slate of well-researched acquisition opportunities.

Remember that the CIM should be well-organized, professional, and transparent. It should provide a compelling narrative of your business, its trajectory, and its goals, along with enough information to pique investors' interest and encourage them to request further details (while still protecting the company's proprietary information). Also, ensure the language is understandable and compelling even to those who may not specialize in your business's market segment.

It is crucial that your team combs the document word by word, making sure that the fonts are the same on every page, the page numbers line up exactly, the colors are exact matches, etc. You need perfection here.

You also need concision—aim for twenty-five slides. I cannot tell you how many companies I see with eighty-slide decks. Don't do it! Even if you are completely convinced that every bit of information needs to be there, cut it down. This attention to detail will elevate the professionalism and impact of your investment materials, and can make a profound difference when it comes to the financing you receive.

Finding Investors

Once you have your CIM ready, the next challenge is initiating investor outreach. Many entrepreneurs face uncertainty about the best approach to what boils down to asking for money. When I advise clients to begin with their own networks, they are often surprised to find they know more potential investors than they think. Don't hesitate to start by diving into professional networking platforms like LinkedIn, AngelList, and Crunchbase, as well as any new ones that have become hot since the drafting of this book, to start compiling a list of prospective investors aligned with your venture. Reach out to existing contacts for referrals and introductions. To curate this list, engage in thorough reviews of previous investments in your focus area, considering factors such as size and terms.

Aim for a targeted directory of one hundred or so potential investors, including venture capital firms, private equity firms, angel investors, and family offices. From that list, you will cull the total down to align with your venture's focus and size.

I won't go into the gory details of what you'll see during your fundraise. All I can suggest is to rest up—and that now is no time for thin skin. Working with investors can open up opportunities that otherwise are only dreams, but it can be a taxing process. Stay calm, put your head down, and keep your eye on the Destination.

You Got the Money!

Great news! As a result of your careful and strategic efforts, you succeeded! You can do a little jumping for joy, but keep your wits about you. It is at this point that I have seen companies, blinded by the cash in the bank, blow through their Guardrails and head directly off the edge of the cliff, never to be heard from again. It's more important than ever at this point to keep that Destination in sight, and to carry with you your company's commitment to Good.

Reflection Questions

Once more, get your leadership team together for this one. Brainstorming is an effective way to answer these questions. It's also good to engage your entire team, as some may have valuable perspectives on capital requirements and how to best use the proceeds. But more than that—it really is good to have your entire team know what goes into raising capital. Most find it's not a process they are eager to repeat and are therefore a little more aware of spending.

Sit down with your team and answer the following questions:

- Does your company have a capital strategy?

- If not, how soon can you gather your people and design one?

- If so, does that strategy allow you plenty of runway, or are you waiting for the economy to turn, the market to improve, or some other outside factor?

- Who do you know in your close network who could invest, or at the very least help guide you through your capital raise?

- If the answer to any of the previous questions relates to the lottery or the death of a rich uncle, please reset your Guardrails and develop an actual plan.

CHAPTER 7

Building a Team

People want to know they matter, and they want to be treated
as people. That's the new talent contract.

—Pamela Stroko,
HCM Practitioner, Author and Keynote Speaker

With money in the bank, you can finally start to flesh out your team. It's a thrilling moment in your company's development—and one that requires you keep from becoming overly exhilarated. Stay on course using Guardrails to keep yourself steadily aimed at your Destination.

As we get into the nitty gritty of your hiring process, it's important to acknowledge that forming your company's team is a complex process, and it tends to whack you with surprises. You may find highly qualified folks from within your trusted circle, and you may also discover the people best suited to fill positions are hovering beyond the industry you currently occupy. But if you're extending your net creatively, get ready to meet your share of weirdos—and not the Expo West kind with whom you might deeply resonate. So, prepare yourself for a wild ride.

At Ganeden, we knew what type of person we needed on the team, but unfortunately—or fortunately, as we found out—the industry all-stars were skeptical of a spore-forming probiotic supplier. And they were even more skeptical when they saw that we already had a line of supplements in the market under our own brand. So, the search began for individuals with the attitudes and skillsets needed to help the company reach its Destination—people outside of the traditional channels.

I knew my first steps were to lock in a few different elements, namely the infrastructure and systems to support our business, as well as a marketing and PR program to spread the message. Luckily, I had a friend who was a perfect hybrid of selling and operational skills, so he was team member number one for Ganeden Labs. Shortly after that came our marketing manager, and we were off to the races. Neither of these team members came from the natural products industry, but they both had the right skill set and more importantly the right attitude for what we were about to undertake. We shared a CFO/COO and VP of Science with the consumer products business, but otherwise we were running on our own. The Ganeden Labs team started setting up the CRM, testing procedures, sampling processes, and everything else you could think of to get us ready to hit the ground running as soon as our safety & regulatory (in this case GRAS) work was completed by the VP of Science.

While we were making great progress in laying the groundwork with processes and trying to drum up commercial interest, we decided it would be best to hire a dedicated sales rep to add to the team, as we were starting to see how long the sales cycle could be. Knowing that the reps in our industry with the thickest rolodexes were sticking to their cushy corporate jobs, we once again set out to find an outlier.

I interviewed half a dozen people out of the fifty or so resumes we received, with the only two real qualifications being: (1) they had to live in or around Cleveland so they could work in the office with the rest of the team, and (2) they had to have successfully sold something on a B2B basis. And wow, did we see diversity in people's qualifications. From people selling truck parts to Mary Kay representatives, the Cleveland area was not a hotbed for experienced ingredient sales professionals, but there were some characters, that's for sure.

One of the six I interviewed met me for coffee, only to tell me immediately that he had a phobia of flying but that he didn't mind driving anywhere. Knowing that fact, I jokingly mentioned that we expected to see a sizable number of opportunities on the West Coast, as well as in Colorado, Florida, and New Jersey. His eager response was "Like I said, I love to drive, and I get all of my calls done while I'm on the road." On the road?! I thought, "Wow. Driving to Seattle . . . from Cleveland." He was a nice enough guy, but the travel thing was a bit of a hitch.

The rest of the interviews were their own versions of peculiar. That is, until a young man who was selling used medical equipment came in to interview and had the attitude and friendly demeanor I was looking for. He talked about how he got to know people and kept notes on their business cards to remind him of things like how many kids they had, where they went to school, what sports teams they followed, and so on. He seemed like a good fit, so we asked for references and let him know we would get back to him. The next day I ran a background check and as a formality I called his manager, who knew he was looking for work, and he gave a positive reference. But then something happened that had never happened to me before or since. "Ya know," said the manager, "he'd do an excellent job for you, but do you know who would knock it out of the park for a company like yours? *Me!*" This guy was trying to steal a job opportunity from one of his employees for whom he was supposed to be providing a reference!

Suffice to say I did not offer the job to the manager. Instead, I made an offer to the actual applicant, who accepted immediately.

And that was it—we were a team of four with a few people from the consumer products side to help us get established with our supplier and check our regulatory boxes. This team of four was the foundation of what would ultimately become the value engine for Ganeden. You'll have your own series of unusual encounters as you find the right people to make up your core team. What follows are some essential strategies to use along the way.

Hiring Basics

So, what really is hiring? I mean—*really.*

First, let me say what it is *not.* When we make Good hiring decisions, we are not acquiring "resources," "FTEs (Full Time Equivalents)," or worse, "warm bodies." And I have heard all those terms used referring to actual human beings with feelings, families, and unique sets of skills. When we hire someone, Guardrails should be set to ensure that the individual is filling a key role. If it is determined that the role is not key to building long-term value for the company, then *do not fill that role.* And if a truly important role *is* being filled, it is your task to find exactly the right human being—the right complex, layered, whole person—to do that specific job.

As leaders, we have responsibilities to our team, customers, partners, investors, and, most of all, the people we are hiring. Companies hire a "resource" to fill a role, relocate that "resource" (and their families, of course) across the country—or the globe—only to find, a year or so later, that this "resource" is no longer needed. Then, of course, said "resource" is unceremoniously eliminated as part of a restructuring, right-sizing, or some other corporate initiative meant to cut cost and help executives make their bonus. This is not a Good hiring practice. And let's remember that Goodness is half of the Guardrailing equation. When people are the focus, any decision that affects them should be considered from all perspectives—including the person affected the most, and with Goodness being the most crucial factor.

Hiring is a huge responsibility that involves finding the right person to fill an important need, as well as forming a team of individuals that is greater than the sum of its parts. Individuals who are all willing and excited to be on this journey together, who share the company's values, and who clearly understand what the Destination is. Those hired must be empowered to act both as individuals and as team members. This ensures that the team is continuously working together to focus on the Destination, while at the same time enjoying the journey—however long it lasts—from start to finish. Of course, there will always be bumps on the roads, and there will always be people who do not make the full journey with you. But as you turn your attention to hiring, I encourage you to take the following guidelines into consideration:

Hire slow, fire fast. I have heard this said plenty of times before, and I have said it repeatedly myself. Although the process can be time-consuming, do not rush the filling of positions. Make sure that each individual hiring is necessary, and evaluate your decisions to be certain they align with your specific Guardrails (the unique aims and end goal) of the department they will be part of, as well as the overall company's commitments to Destination and Good. Obviously, your company will benefit from you taking the time to find employees who will truly enrich the team—and everyone will be well served when you avoid the many potential problems that come with rushing through the process and hiring the wrong people. However, if you do find that a mistake has been made, don't hesitate to let the new hire go quickly. The less wasted time, the better.

Be strategic about where you find employees. Recruit from within your network whenever possible, as these individuals typically come highly recommended and may have worked with you or a close colleague in the past. It is always best when you know the individual personally. Second best is when you can speak to a trusted contact who is much more likely to provide an honest reference versus a brush-off reference.

If you can't find someone through your direct network, make sure that you have excellent relationships with executive recruiters and staffing companies that specifically focus on your industry. For example, if you are trying to hire an account manager to sell ingredients, make sure you know the specific recruiters who work within that space. It can be very well worth the time and money to use a search firm if you are hiring for a position but don't have someone available in your network.

Check background. Far too many companies rely solely on references rather than formal background checks. References typically will not tell you about someone's DUI, side business, or bankruptcy—but background checks will. Even if it costs a couple hundred dollars extra each time, run a thorough background check on every single person you hire. If you don't, important bits of a person's history can be missed—including information that would have certainly prevented the individual from being hired by the company.

Be honest. Since your objective is to sell the business at some point in the future, let every single person that you interview know that that is the Destination. During interviews, tell candidates that the company was designed to be sold to generate the greatest amount of value for the investors as well as the team. That means that one day, they will all either be working for a PE firm/larger multinational company . . . or simply be out of a job. But while on this journey, and at the end of the journey, every single contributing individual will be rewarded for their work.

Compensate fairly. Develop a compensation plan that rewards the team for their successes. Commissions motivate sales professionals, and bonuses motivate everyone. Keep base salaries reasonable and keep variable compensation (for those on variable comp plans) unlimited. In my experience, virtually every time a company has eliminated commission or bonus plans, there is a marked drop in individual contributions. This, of course, requires the company to hire additional staff to do what a smaller, properly motivated staff should be able to accomplish by themselves. I have spent a good bit of time over the course of my career designing compensation plans and know that there is not a one-size-fits-all model. But what I do know is that often the right team is motivated by being rewarded financially for their hard work, and everything else is just icing on the cake.

Consider culture. If you hire an individual, regardless of their stellar qualifications, and they turn out to disrupt the culture you have so mindfully built for your organization, there are two choices: work with the individual to quickly remedy their deficiencies or remove that person from the company without hesitation. Company cultures are unique. Like a corporate fingerprint. It never ceases to surprise me how different one company's culture may be from another even though the companies may be seemingly similar. Observe this phenomenon the next time you are at a trade show or visiting a business. But again— culture. It's a hard-fought battle to establish a company's culture, ethics, and "vibe." Having someone on the team that doesn't fit in can be a devastating distraction. The person may accomplish their tasks, achieve their numbers, ship the right quantity of products, and show up for work without fail, but if the attitude they bring is not in alignment with the business, all aspects of the organization suffer.

As in all choices, think Destination. When hiring a new team member, take careful consideration as to what will happen to that individual when you sell the business. Will that person's role add unique value to the acquiring business, or will they wind up losing their job because they are in a position that is likely to be already filled in the acquiring business? You may have the capital and the desire to hire individuals who can remove some of the work from a certain member of the team. If so, determine whether you could restructure that existing employee's position so that they do not need the additional help, or compensate that employee in such a way that they are paid to do the extra work, rather than hiring an additional individual who will ultimately be let go after the acquisition.

A company can have a nice exit, leaving senior executives and investors happy and well rewarded, but what if Goodness is ignored while hiring? Imagine walking through the grocery store after the sale of your company and encountering a former employee who dedicated years of hard work to help you reach your Destination, but who received no financial benefit from the sale and lost their job due to position redundancy. You've got a shiny new car and a vacation home in Hilton Head, while they are trudging through the cereal aisle with a fistful of clipped coupons. Simply put, make sure that you have the right team and only the right team.

Nepotism? Many companies have strict policies against nepotism, and I agree that having family members or even close friends reporting to each other is typically a bad idea. But in the right environment, nepotism can be awesome. I have consulted with companies where spouses worked together and have seen them perform fabulously with zero conflicts. At various times in the past, my father, daughters, and wife all worked or consulted for one of our companies, and not once did I regret working with any of them.

So long as the individual is well qualified for a given position, a different level of accountability and partnership occurs when family members work in a business. The team succeeds or fails together. And besides—imagine the benefit to the company if your team members are brainstorming over dinner, on vacation, or even while settling in for bed? However you approach close or familial relationships in your company, it is crucial to set Guardrails so that intimate connections creatively nourish the business, while they maintain the support and breathing room they need to remain healthy.

Titles. Finally, titles. A business typically starts off with a core team of individuals with domain expertise. Increasingly, traditional titles are being replaced by descriptive ones (chief or account manager), or no unique titles are being used at all. For example, some companies refer to everyone as an associate, which creates a feeling of equality. But the more complex an organization is, the more confusing positions can be regarding hierarchy. So, if your company chooses the path of avoiding specific titles, the decision should be made with eyes open to potential pitfalls—and the company should set up the structure from the start, as it is exceedingly difficult to change that once titles have been handed out. While it is great for everyone to feel equal by being called team members, associates, sprites, or whatever they are called, there has to be some way to indicate to the outside world who holds decision-making authority and who does not. A team of associates is great until a customer wants to "speak to the manager" and there is no one with that role or title. Just be certain that roles are defined if titles are not.

And on top of all that, there's also another area of hiring that deserves its own section.

Developing a Commercial Team

Commercial team formation has a few of its own peculiarities, and it's worth zeroing in on the Guardrail work required to do it successfully.

When you're developing your commercial team, let's imagine that your first thought is to reach out to some of the experienced sales professionals who work for competitive suppliers and see if they would be interested in joining your startup. You might do the normal networking—say that at an industry event, you meet several salespeople who are very experienced at selling into your market. Maybe you've had optimistic conversations with these professionals.

And then—whammo! You are hit with unexpected and confusing responses like these: "The market is pretty saturated with similar products." "How big is your marketing budget and can you sell into China?" "Our clients are really happy to be able to buy a majority of their ingredients from a single supplier. Single-ingredient suppliers (or whatever your company aims to sell) are going to soon be a thing of the past."

Disciplined, Guardrail-guided decision-making can cut through the confusion.

Using Guardrails to Hire a Commercial Team

So, you aren't sure what to make of the complexities of the market, and you need experienced salespeople in the field. As usual, orienting toward the Destination, in large and small ways, offers a quick return to clarity.

What is your end goal in hiring for these positions, and for that matter, how will the hires affect the company overall? Keeping the Destination clearly in your sights you can get a better sense of the type of person you want to hire for each role. You may seek salespeople with a background in your product area due to the complexity of the product. Or you may find that hiring people from outside industries wouldn't hurt, and in fact could really help. What does matter is finding sales experts who have the right attitude and drive. For example, say you are selling a food ingredient that has a specialized use in dairy applications. In that case, you may want to ensure that the account manager you hire has experience and familiarity with dairy food science, and that she is familiar with the technical aspects of the technology. But beyond that, fit is key.

Whether or not you find salespeople with content-related backgrounds, the general hiring concerns apply. In addition to the items on the previous bulleted list, it's important to consider whether they align with your company's commitment to Good, and whether they are excited to be working in service of the company's Destination. And once again, do they fit in comfortably with the company culture?

As you expand the commercial team by hiring account managers, a marketing manager, a communications manager, and perhaps a sales and marketing coordinator, your business is progressing, readying itself to ship your product or deliver your service. Depending on how you assemble your commercial team, the success of individuals unfamiliar with the industry may even impress investors and advisers.

Through strict use of the Guardrails, you can build a commercial team that on paper shouldn't work but in person dazzles with skill and success.

Trip Test

Confession: I do not consider myself a skillful technical interviewer. I typically do not follow interview questions and do not try to trip individuals up by asking trick or leading questions. My interviewing approach would not impress a traditional HR director. But the way I interview tends to work for the kinds of companies that matter to me. I like to get to know the person as an individual, see how they react to my personality and the personalities of those around them. I watch how they handle themselves in social situations. And I prefer to do interviews face-to-face in an office space, or better yet a restaurant or coffee shop. For me, face-to-face interviews are nonnegotiable.

Over the years I have developed what I call the "trip test." (Note: This test only comes into play when we have already established that an individual is a good technical fit for a position.) When I am interviewing someone over a cup of coffee, chatting about their interests, I imagine myself on a trip with this individual. We share plane rides, meals, and rental car rides and spend every waking moment together for a week or two. I ask myself if I would look forward to traveling with this person, or would it be agony? The answer makes the hiring decision amazingly simple. If I would not want to spend a week with them, more than likely others won't want to either, so it's time be extra judicious when considering this candidate for a given position. I haven't always followed my own advice and have hired individuals who look great on paper but drove me—and others—crazy. The failure rate of these individuals is significantly higher than the rate for those who passed the trip test.

You may come up with your own imaginary scenarios, but I do encourage you to envision yourself working closely with a candidate, taking into account the nuances of interpersonal interactions. How do they rate in your fantasy situations? Does the thought of hashing out business challenges elbow-to-elbow in high-pressure circumstances make you wince? Or does it make you smile?

Big Picture: Lead with Heart

In the startup hustle, you'll be spending long hours with your coworkers—sometimes more than with your family and friends. You'll learn about your coworkers' financial hardships, substance abuse, mental health issues, and the list goes on and on. Is it your job to find them help? Technically no, but it's a Good decision to do so.

Remember, a "Good decision" not only serves the immediate objective but also aligns with the broader values of the individual and business. For this reason, in team formation—as in all areas of your business—considering a decision's Goodness is as important as considering its ability to get you to your Destination.

Here's an example. A few years into our work with Ganeden, we were regularly launching products with food and beverage customers, and decided it was time to bring on another early career sales rep. After interviewing for a month or so, we hired a delightful young woman from Cleveland who had been selling chocolate for a candy company for fundraisers. I figured if she could be successful doing that, she was going to be a rock star for us. She had been working with us for a few months and was doing well, but seemed like she was struggling a bit. I had a brief hallway chat with one of the other team members where it was mentioned that our new sales rep was also working a second job to make ends meet.

The morning after that discovery, I met with the young woman and told her I'd make her a deal. If she quit her second job, I would pay her what she was making at her other job—an extra two thousand dollars per month—as a draw against future commissions for one year. The only catch was, if she resigned within that year, she would have to pay it back—but otherwise, it would simply be a prepayment on commissions I expected to be paying her in a few months anyway. I've seen situations like this go one of two ways: Either the individual accepts the offer and works like crazy to prove I was making a Good decision, or they say no thanks and are gone in a few months. Fortunately for us, her choice was behind door number one. Not only did she pay the full amount of her draw back during her first year, but she exceeded it.

A small, short-term investment in someone with potential can often pay dividends in the long term. If you are an entre-preneurial leader, I believe your relationship with your team should transcend the typical risk-management approach that HR often uses. I have found myself playing roles ranging from coach and mentor to wellness and event coordinator. Of course, you will have to play "manager" when action is needed to get someone back on track (or off the team), but really, your role is about helping and supporting the people you work with professionally—and occasionally, personally.

And Last, Invest in Employee Well-Being

At Ganeden, we installed gyms and offered personal training so our staff could get in a workout and shower without having to schlep to a gym before or after work—or worse, during lunch. We offered storytelling workshops, brought in mindfulness and positive psychology experts, and attended stand-up comedy shows.

I've also had to navigate some situations where the management team had to shift Guardrails to help individuals who were having family health emergencies or facing financial issues, and we have sent individuals to programs to support their professional and personal development. In Guardrail terms, these were always Good decisions.

A mentally and physically healthy team is a happy team, and a happy team is a productive team. And more than that—it's a team you love to be around.

Reflection Questions

- If you sell your company, which individuals on your team would be hard to replace by the acquiring firm, and who would not make the cut?

- Do you have a commercial team that is meeting the needs of your company, is happy, and is loved by their customers? If so—excellent job! High-five yourself and take a nap.

- If not, what might be the problem? (Hint: look at compensation, autonomy, and management.)

- Develop a list of action items that will support your commercial team's success.

CHAPTER 8

Avoid Unnecessary Science Detours

Have values and principles that you can articulate that you're
willing to fight for, and that means something to you and
that you considered. Simultaneously, be ready to morph and
upgrade yourself in an authentic way as you go.

—Ben Goodwin, CEO, Olipop

If your business is built around content or a product or
service that requires no scientific data, you can skip to the
next chapter. But if you've got a new ingredient you intend to
sell, these pages are important, so read on.

You may have a growing team that consists of R&D scientists,
a quality manager, and an individual who would oversee the
day-to-day lab operations. And you may be thinking it's time to
embark on a slew of clinical trials. After all, that's how to gather
interest and gain credibility for what you've innovated, right?

If you think that you need to start with multisite, multiple end
point studies, you are on the brink of making one of the most
common science mistakes I see startups make. It is often an
earnest, well-planned decision, but it's one that can devour pre-
cious time and capital. It's the big, fancy "gold standard" clinical
trial, involving prestigious universities and many participants
and costing a million dollars or more. These drawn-out, massive,

and wildly expensive studies often do not produce results you can discuss for a year or more—if ever. And this simply doesn't work for a scrappy startup.

It's easy to stumble down this road. At Ganeden, three of us took a road trip to see a potential customer. It was the third or fourth visit to meet with this hybrid pharma/consumer product company, and we were there to share the results of a trial we ran at the suggestion of their science team. We proudly presented the results and the statistical significance that our trial showed for our probiotic's ability to support immune health. The data was fantastic. For you statistics geeks, the trial showed the statistical significance of $p < 0.05$—which to you non-stats geeks means it tells us how likely it is that the results they found could just be due to random chance. When they say "$p < 0.05$," it means the chance of the results being random is less than 5 percent. In other words, there's a pretty low probability that the ingredient, in this case BC^{30}, isn't making a difference.

During the meeting, we were visibly excited that we met their statistical threshold and did everything asked of us to show that the ingredient would create a measurable effect for their consumers. Suddenly, one of the company's senior scientists raised his hand and said, "That's all well and good, and we congratulate you on a successful trial, but we only accept trials with an n [that is the number of subjects in a trial] of 300." I informed them that we were able to see significance with less than forty subjects and were not going to spend millions of dollars simply to show the same results. We were at a stalemate: We ran the study, it was a success by all statistical measures, and yet their corporate policy (which we were unaware of at the onset of the project) was not met, and the project was dead. At this, we thanked them, excused ourselves, marked that opportunity as being Closed/Lost in our CRM, and went off to lick our wounds. We could have spent the money to run the new clinical, but why would we spend more than ten times as much to make the same claim? Our trial allowed us to support the claim that was worded "Supports Immune Health," which is the same claim we would have used for a study with three hundred, three thousand, or even ten thousand people.

I see this dilemma often. Companies run oversized studies to make basic claims, with the decisions being made around the clinical typically being driven by ego, a desire to publish in a top-tier journal, or a lack of understanding of how claims work outside of the world of pharmaceuticals. The extra expense doesn't move them one step closer to their Destination, and according to the principles of Guardrailing, we should not choose to run a study larger than necessary to gain statistical significance. As a side note, our opinion was: If it takes three hundred or more people to reach statistical significance, the ingredient isn't likely to provide an effect that can be readily felt by the average consumer and therefore that claim area should be reconsidered.

So, how do you keep clear of these cringy wastes of time?

Meet the Naturals Scientist

First, let's look at the unique world of scientists and researchers in the natural products space. They may have done their graduate work at prestigious universities and dreamed of developing the next blockbuster drug, only to realize that they just did not relate to the people and pharma industries that were developing that next blockbuster drug. Our industry tends to have smaller science teams, teams that are often made up of innovators who are willing to try approaches that may not be acceptable in the world of big biotech or pharma.

Over the years, I have worked with gut health researchers who have followed livestock around a field to obtain fecal samples or run proof-of-concept studies using the team members at the company to generate data to steer future trials. They are scientific mavericks who spend less money to publish more papers supporting claims. They gain regulatory approvals globally through pioneering uses of data and develop manufacturing processes that are less expensive and far less complex than what we might otherwise see in other industries.

Savvy Science

As mentioned above, it is quite easy to fall into the "study trap" with a research trial and find yourself watching months pass as your expensive and time-consuming study crawls along with you standing idly by, fingers crossed, as you wait for a positive outcome. Fortunately, there are now contract research organizations (CROs) around the globe that will design, conduct, and manage clinical trials for smaller companies. But before you pick up the phone and start planning trials with a CRO, let's take a moment to review your research Guardrails and determine your needs.

Destination question: How will research trials help you reach your Destination?

Example: As an ingredient provider selling on a B2B basis, your key selling proposition is the claims your customers can make based on your science. Typically, customers are concerned that the studies support claims and are published. To support your journey to your Destination, ensure that the studies you arrange support claims that can legally be made on the packages of your customers' products—and the more of these, the merrier. Multiple targeted claim-support studies will drive value for you and your customers. And if the potential claim can't be made in the market your customers are selling into? Do not waste money on the study.

Good decision question: What parameters of ethics should you use to evaluate proposed research?

Example: It goes without saying (but I'll say it anyway) that doing trials that are reviewed and blessed by an IRB (Institutional Review Board) is an absolute must. Ensure that the study is looking at clinical endpoints that will benefit the end consumer and that the claim being made is available at a cost that will meet the commercial and logistical needs of your customers. You are in the business of doing Good and improving the quality of life of those who use your products—keep this in mind at all times.

Engaging a CRO

A two-year, $700,000 trial with a university might be well beyond your emerging company's timeline and financial reach. Put another way, it may cause you to veer so far off the road to your Destination that your company flies right off a financial cliff.

After pondering the prospect of an extensive trial through the lens of the central Guardrail principles, you might realize you don't need an expensive university tie-in after all. Guided by Guardrails, your next step may be to connect with a CRO, perhaps one recommended by a colleague.

A typical CRO's approach is a straightforward risk-management process. It might start with a proof-of-concept trial using validated models (such as gut models) to show that the expected clinical benefits would be seen, and this initial trial would inform the claim areas and clinical end points the company should focus on. After successfully running a model to determine the most prominent benefits, the CRO may suggest testing an open-label pilot trial to identify the model's observed positive outcomes. Those initial trials would enable the CRO to determine the number of subjects needed to achieve statistical significance in a placebo-controlled study and target specific end points where they are most likely to see positive benefits.

This methodology, although intricate, is aimed at generating publishable data with reduced risk. It is the kind of strategy CROs specialize in, and it tends to be both significantly faster and significantly less expensive than multi–end point studies with a more shotgun approach.

An added benefit: CROs can have relationships with relevant online journals as well, which may facilitate the publication of the clinical trial, providing crucial support for your company's claims. Remember, publishing positive outcomes is the goal, and speed is of the essence.

This systematic approach, driven by Guardrails, will reaffirm the value of producing cost-effective clinical data on your ingredient, and your business will enjoy increased stability from the success born of keeping its eyes on the Destination, that essential North Star.

Navigating Ethics at the Research Phase

Often, a team must consider decisions that solely impact short-term objectives—frequently to the detriment of the ultimate Destination. It can be easy to agree on an action that might make things appear smoother in the short term, but the choice you make may impair your ability to reach your goal in the future.

A potential customer of Ganeden once asked me to allow them to use a small percentage of the clinically validated serving size of an ingredient, so that they could make the cost of the ingredient work with their product. (This actually happened less often than one would think, but when it did, it was usually with a very multinational CPG firm.) We were clear that to make any of the claims we supported, higher levels of the ingredient must be included in each daily serving. To maintain their margins, this customer proposed they would put a fraction in and state on the package that the ingredient was in the product, but they would not make the claims that were supported by the published science. It was a very sizable account, and the opportunity would be very lucrative for our company.

But when I sat down with the account manager, who was extremely excited to close this huge opportunity, I asked her one question: "If your grandmother were to take only one product to support her digestive health, would you recommend this one?" The decision was instantly clear.

The account manager reached back out to the customer to let them know that if they were unwilling or unable to put the clinically documented serving size of this ingredient in their product, we would be unable to work with them. After some back-and-forth, the client was bound and determined to launch the product anyway, which they did with an alternate supplier, and the product was in—and *out*—of the market in less than a year.

These types of decisions, at least in my mind, are simple. Focus on doing Good one hundred percent of the time, and you fulfill your promise to the end customer one hundred percent of the time. You may miss out on large revenue opportunities, but you will be able to sleep at night, and this level of integrity will be rewarded at the finish line. And your North Star, your Destination—that end goal you've got in your sights—shines only more brightly with each of your company's courageous acts of integrity. Potential acquiring entities will know your company as trustworthy, for that reputation will grow with every choice you make for the greater good.

Guardrailing Must Guide Your Research Decisions

Science to support a product's claims can be a huge investment. But if made wisely, using the parameters of Guardrailing, critical errors can be avoided.

After exploring many different avenues, we determined that since we were running clinical trials for the specific purpose of supporting structure-function claims that would appear on the packages and marketing material for foods, beverages, and supplements, we needed a plan to ensure the most bang for our limited bucks.

We decided to use a very disciplined approach to new scientific areas where we would take initial lab data that supported our hypothesis, and work with an independent Contract Research Organization (CRO) to design a cost-effective model to prove the concept. After successful completion of the model, we would review the data and find the data that best supported the claim we were shooting for and run an open-label human pilot trial on that endpoint. After the pilot, we would review the data with a biostatistician who would determine how many subjects we would need in a Randomized Controlled Trial (RCT) to ensure statistical significance. If the number was low enough, which to us indicated that the average consumer would feel the impact, we would run the study. If the number of subjects required was higher than what we felt we could justify from an ROI perspective, we went back to the drawing board knowing we had just dodged an extremely expensive bullet.

It's how we ran and planned studies at Ganeden, and honestly, I feel it's the way companies in our space should all run trials. Why run a million- (or more) dollar immune study when at the end of the day the claim that you can make such as "Supports the Immune System" can be supported with a $100,000 to $200,000 study? I don't know why, but I see it all the time.

Reflection Questions

- In generating data to support your products, either in-house or with outside resources, does the outcome of your work align within the Guardrails set by the company?

- If not, how can you move the Guardrails relating to research to ensure that you are on the path to your Destination?

CHAPTER 9

Continuous Assessment

I value self-discipline but creating systems that make it next to
impossible to misbehave is more reliable than self-control.

—TIM FERRIS, AUTHOR, PODCAST HOST

The natural products world is like a business version of
Burning Man. Our wonderfully wild community of
individuals, companies, and even investors are having a fantastic
time working to make a tall pile of money while also making
a positive impact on society, consumers, and the Earth. I'm
not saying other industries aren't championing Good, but in
naturals, that pursuit is ubiquitous. Our field is known for its
tolerance and acceptance of diverse approaches and personalities.
One need only visit Expo West once to realize that it does not
take a dark blue suit and Johnston Murphy loafers to achieve
your goals, either financially or ethically. It takes passion and
vision. And it takes heart.

Here's the challenge, and I bet you will recognize it: You're
steering your company toward its Destination amid a culture
of doing things differently, but you still must hit the financial
markers that pave the way to your goal. And to determine your
company's relative proximity to that goal, you need to be fully
engaged in assessment.

Assessment, the Old-Fashioned Way

Traditionally, companies use assessment tools with initials like OKRs, MBOs, and KPIs. But do these resources ensure that the company is staying on the path to the Destination? And are there tools to get back on track if things go awry? Or are the tools a company uses simply corporate acronyms symbolizing risk management and employee control?

I have found in my work with a range of businesses that most of these old-school assessment tools and metrics are geared toward identifying poor performers and those who are not following policies and procedures. They do not tend to provide the feedback necessary to support an individual's growth within the organization. Nor do they point out ways the company can improve its relationship with its employees. Additionally, these very specific individual goals are typically set a year or so in advance and do not take into consideration the natural evolution of a business. Often, objectives that seemed very relevant in November are irrelevant in June, but the company is stuck on the objective and has to work around its irrelevance.

Assessment Using Guardrailing

Keeping your business on course begins with a revenue forecast. This prediction should be both reasonable and thoroughly examined by a team ready to adjust financial Guardrails based on market dynamics, industry changes, and any unforeseen factors that could impact the company's trajectory.

Being a bit of a tech enthusiast (a.k.a. a nerd), I've leveraged technology throughout my career to automate and streamline tasks. I place great emphasis on straightforward metrics that resonate with everyone, and I believe in openly sharing company goals and progress with the entire team. I suspect my approach will keep productivity on track for your company. It works like this:

Every week, the entire team receives a concise revenue report. This ensures everyone is on the same page, providing a clear snapshot of where the business stands according to the forecast presented to the board and investors. Additionally, on a monthly basis, a detailed document circulates among the commercial and management teams. It breaks down the performance of each account manager, account by account, offering a comprehensive view of how the company is measuring up against the forecast.

Some company cultures would consider this open style of communication to be punitive, with the company reporting on the sales success, or lack thereof, of every account manager. I would counter that peer pressure *promotes* comradery. It encourages team members to pull together to help one another excel.

When I initially began experimenting with this type of transparency, I was both startled and pleased to observe the results. I assumed that at these meetings, the star account managers—those consistently at 125 percent of forecast—would be angry that they were carrying the company or condescending to their lesser performing colleagues, but my experience has been quite the opposite. The overperformers tend to support underperformers to help them achieve their goals, considering that the goal of the individual rolls up into the goals of the team and affects everyone.

Individual contributors who are not reaching their goals—and who are upset by the fact that their colleagues know it—have two choices. They can either work harder and rely upon the resources within the company, or they can make the choice to leave the organization. My experience has shown that the first option is the one taken much of the time, especially if proper financial incentives are put in place to compensate contributors for reaching the goals they set for themselves.

From a leadership perspective, it is crucial to track the work being put in by commercial teams—and the results of that work. Understanding a company's sales process is also especially important, as the conversion of leads tends to correlate directly with the actions taken to move an account from the beginning of the pipeline to the position where they are a customer. Often, an account manager may not be achieving their forecast, but the employee's activity shows that they are working hard and doing all the right things. It is by monitoring the details that you can identify where help is needed, rather than simply judging the individual by their revenue generation. Properly focused activity typically turns into cash when sales are involved. Sometimes it just takes a while.

The benefits of handling assessment in this way are both ethical and practical. Of course, measuring performance fairly also honors the primary Guardrailing principle of doing Good. And in practice, company culture thrives when team members aren't operating in fear that their efforts will meet with unfair consequences. This approach moves the business as a whole toward its Destination.

Dashboard Monitoring

For many years, I have monitored commercial activities and customer satisfaction through a single dashboard that is automatically generated by a CRM. Throughout my career, and at various organizations, the use of this dashboard, which is reviewed daily, has typically taken me no more than five minutes each morning—but the insights are well worth the efforts.

Key metrics I measure are (by account manager and summed to show companywide results):

- New leads
- Newly signed NDAs (Non-Disclosure Agreements)
- Samples sent
- Newly signed purchase agreements
- Calls made
- Emails sent
- Face-to-face meetings held
- New pipeline opportunities
- Opportunity movement in pipeline
- All open leads
- All open opportunities
- Total accounts

This dashboard, coupled with the weekly revenue report and the monthly account manager 'actual versus forecast' report, has given me great insight into how the commercial team is performing and how the company is doing as a business. Couple these with basic financials (P&L, balance sheet, and cash flow statement), and you have a particularly good indication of how things are going from a commercial perspective. Positive results are typically an indication that your Guardrails are set appropriately; i.e., performance metrics are reasonable and achievable. In contrast, problems revealed in the data can suggest needed adjustments to your Guardrails. As an example of a Guardrail adjustment, I was digging into the daily dashboard reviews and assessing the number of calls a particular account member would make over the course of the week. We found that calls were being placed but the messages were being returned by the potential customer via email, thus showing mediocre performance from a call perspective. In this case, I adjusted my Guardrails to give less weight to the number of calls placed and more weight to interactions (whether email, text, conversations) in general.

Meeting with Your Team

I encourage your company to implement these additional actions:

On a weekly basis. Hold staff meetings that range from twenty to thirty minutes. Have attendees give three examples of positive things they are working on, and also have them ask for help where they need it. Include the sales and marketing teams, the operations team, the R&D team, and any team members supporting those efforts. Before the meetings, leadership should review the dashboard, and everyone attending should receive the revenue report, so all are aware of where the company is in relationship to the forecast. The weekly meeting also offers a good opportunity to discuss any big wins or any issues with customers, so that the team can decide how to handle challenges and repeat successes.

On a monthly basis. Add in a meeting for a monthly performance report that indicates how account managers are doing, as compared to their forecast. It is this report that typically leads to fruitful conversation with individuals who are either performing very well or not measuring up to the plan.

In typical business settings, there are a lot of sales managers, CEOs, and others who are responsible for business teams, and who do weekly meetings with their sales teams on an individual basis. Indeed, your company may operate this way. I find this approach to be time-consuming and counterproductive. Again, consider the company's Destination. Why would you want your customer-facing team members to be spending their time drafting reports, sitting in meetings, filling out forms, or doing other administrative work if the real value is generated when they are communicating directly with current and prospective customers?

On a quarterly basis. Hold board meetings where all of the data we've discussed is synthesized into simple slides, and where the relevant managers are tasked with summarizing their accomplishments and challenges. You may wish to have the senior management members responsible for functional business areas attend these meetings, as their presence shows the board that your team is made up of more than just executive leadership—that the company consists of individual contributors without whom the business would not be a success. The prep for the board meeting provides all the information the team needs to gauge how the company is doing on a quarterly basis. Leadership and team members can then provide board members with an update that inspires confidence that the company is well on its way to achieving its goal. See the next section for targeted guidance on board meetings. They are a special kind of animal, and they warrant your full attention.

On an annual basis. Businesses should go through an intense budgeting/forecasting period. Budgeting starts in October, with the goal being to have the budget and full revenue forecast pinned down in November, or at the very latest early December. The forecast as it relates to sales should be generated by the individuals personally responsible for generating those sales. It is valuable for companies to have compensation plans that incentivize people to hit their forecast, but it is also important to incentivize for goals that are a stretch beyond layups. Account managers should go account by account and opportunity by opportunity, and forecast the sales on a month-by-month basis for the following year—all with direct input from the current or potential customer. The budgeting/forecasting period serves as a vital opportunity to give your business a careful review for both opportunities (and how they will be handled) and challenges that will need to be addressed in the coming year. Needed changes and next steps will be illuminated, with that clearly defined Destination shimmering ahead, inspiring your company's unceasing efforts toward success.

Board Meetings

It is common for company leadership to approach board meetings with at least a twinge of anxiety. If you aren't sure how best to handle those quarterly meetings, read on. Following are strategies for making the most of these opportunities to hear from the people you have enlisted precisely because they bring insight and expertise.

Get materials to board members at least three days before the meeting—longer if a weekend is involved.

Come into the meeting well rested and open to suggestions. The night before a board meeting is not the time for the executive team to polish off a bottle of scotch—save the party for after the meeting.

Ask and expect that the board has read the material ahead of time.

Do not go through the slides bullet by bullet. For each functional area that is being reported on (e.g., sales, R&D, marketing, finance), I suggest focusing on three top initiatives to discuss with the board.

Where challenges exist, present them along with potential solutions.

In cases where board input is needed relating to the challenges, and or proposed solutions, it can be useful to ask specifically for board help. They can't read your mind, so if you would like help with specific issues, you usually have to mention it.

Otherwise, use the board more as a governing body and a place to do a sanity check, rather than a group of individuals to depend on for answers.

Allow time for the board to meet without the employees/executive team at the end of the meeting (executive session), and ask the board for feedback afterwards. It's tough, but your board members will likely have loads of experience, and they are there to help the business succeed.

Forecasting for "Ingredient People"

If your product is an ingredient, some special forecasting issues may come into play. The ingredient space can be challenging to forecast, as orders are sometimes placed based on contract manufacturer availability, sell-through at retailers, and a variety of other variables that cannot necessarily be controlled by their ingredient supplier. Make sure account managers build their forecasts with direct input from their customers. I have found that this strategy results in predictions that are far more accurate, with a more thorough understanding of timing and volumes. After all, the information comes from customers; the data is based on real-world conversations, not guesses or wishes.

Many years of experience have shown me that a strong commercial team, with a forecast that has been informed by direct conversations with customers and prospects, will land somewhere around 85 percent of the forecasted goal. (Eighty-five percent is very good, by the way.) Some account managers will have additional revenue added to their individually developed forecast, and others may be encouraged to dial it back to ensure that their goals are reasonable and achievable. Either way, though, the result of this process is a forecast that is typically well in alignment with the business plan that was initially generated and presented to investors. It also typically aligns with the value generation path that guides the company along the journey to the Destination.

At the end of each year, we produce a detailed analysis of actual customer performance versus the original forecast and reward super contributors for their accomplishments. Then, we reset expectations for the new year with a new forecast and a solid, agreed-upon plan. That planning process then has us ready for new challenges, accomplishments, and celebrations, for yet another year well planned and well executed.

However you approach it, make sure you put in place tools for assessment that capture accurate and applicable data without taxing team members to the point of frustration. Both things matter for the success of your business. Doing this part right can contribute quite meaningfully to a positive company culture, as well.

Reflection Questions

- Do you have a single-view dashboard from which you can easily assess the key areas of your business?

- Given the Guardrail guidance in this chapter, do you need to take time to draft one or revise the dashboard you currently use?

- Are you open and transparent with your team about the business's progress toward its Destination?

CHAPTER 10

Destination Reached—The Sale

Stakeholders make up a company. They include all the people
who impact and are impacted by a business. We must honor
them as people first before treating them according to the role
they happen to be playing.

—John Mackey, Co-founder, Whole Foods

I f selling your business is your Destination, and you've used
this book at each part of your path with that goal in mind,
congratulations! You are very close. Feel free to buy that case
of champagne—but don't start popping corks just yet. Your
vigilant attention is as important now as it has been throughout
your journey so far, for the sale process can be every bit as
daunting at the startup phase.

Of course, endgame circumstances can play out in a lot of
different ways. But as with the entirety of your journey, the
point is to hold your Destination at the center of your vision
and to operate in alignment with your company's values—to do
Good—all the way to your exit. Beyond the big-picture Guardrailing and decision-making we've already discussed, a variety
of significant choices will be required as your business moves
toward its sale.

Selling a company is complex. Since many variables exist at this point in the process, let's imagine a particular trajectory for your business and consider the ways that Guardrailing can be used to make the right decisions along the way. This will allow you to see the mechanism of Guardrailing and how it can help your business determine best actions, no matter what final challenges your company faces.

The Decision to Explore Sale

So, let's say that at your Q1 board meeting, the familiar rhythm of updates took a distinctive and exciting turn. Perhaps your company had reached over $5 million in EBITDA the prior year and the team was abuzz with excitement. Maybe your leadership team had estimated that the company had reached the starting point to where you could justify a selling price above $50 million, and your board decided to explore the possibility of selling the business. And let's imagine that inquiries from strategic buyers, venture capital, and private equity firms have become commonplace. So, now, your board opts to meet with investment bankers to determine whether an auction process would be appropriate to maximize your company's value.

Selection of Advisors, Bankers, and Legal Team

As the leader of the organization, you should join forces with a board member with extensive experience in venture capital and investment banking, and vet investment bankers and lawyers together. Although your current business firm may be great, the board favors specialists in mergers, acquisitions, and transactions, so you need to set out to build that team. The mission you've been tasked with: sell your company by year-end.

After a few meetings with anxious bankers, you select a banker with a stellar reputation for running smooth sales processes and achieving better than average results for private sellers. You then make a similar decision for the law firm, and fortunately the bankers and lawyers have worked deals together, and they know what it takes to work together to get deals closed.

Tips that will benefit you at this stage of the sale effort:

- *Take your time.*

- Meet with a variety of bankers and lawyers to find the ones with experience in your market.

- Talk to prior clients and check references.

- If at all possible, bring a veteran advisor with you to meet with these firms, as there are many factors to consider, and making the right decision is very important. Hiring the right bankers and lawyers to guide you through this potentially life-changing pursuit can be the difference between a successful exit and a mediocre one.

- In addition to their qualifications, you should look at which bankers and lawyers you like and trust. You will be spending a great deal of time with these folks over the next several quarters, so you want to make sure you are working with people you enjoy and can count on to patiently guide you through the ins and outs of the process.

- Oh, yeah, and just accept the fact that the fees charged by the best firms are massive. Negotiate, but don't be penny wise and pound foolish.

Data Room and CIM Creation

Once everything has been arranged, the chosen banker and attorney will present their process to the board, gaining approval to kick off the sale. They are likely to estimate the length of time from contract signing to closing (let's say approximately nine months), and they will address the board's expectations as they relate to exit value. Once the timeline and approach have been established, the banker may set up a data room, get to work crafting a Confidential Information Memorandum (CIM), and develop a targeted list of potential buyers.

If you've been paying attention at all, you know that early on in your company's planning stages, your team dreamed of who would buy the business. Years have passed, a tremendous amount of work has gone into building the business, and your initial list of potential buyers has shrunk due to consolidation, but it contains the same players you starry-eyed founders felt would provide the greatest value in a strategic exit. If you're in this position, the bankers you've engaged will doubtless be impressed. The mere fact that your company conducted this exercise at all would indicate to financial representatives that they are working with a sharp, dedicated, and thoughtful group of entrepreneurs. The spoils of Destination-first planning at work!

Outreach and Presentations

An important aspect of selling a business—maybe one of the most important—is the management presentations where the team of the selling company meets with the team of the acquiring party. At these meetings, both teams will get to ask and answer questions, get a feel for the dynamics of the team, and see things face-to-face, beyond the CIM and data in the data room. It is here that the buyer not only determines whether what they are seeing on paper is real, but also meets the management team to determine fit. All too often, I have seen management presentations that were performed by the CEO with input from the CFO—while the team members who would remain with the business to operate it and continue its growth after the sale are left sitting in their offices, wondering what is happening. This approach leads buyers to think that the business is largely led and controlled by the CEO and CFO (or whomever they invite into the presentation), and it often leaves them feeling that the company lacks the depth of talent to run the business after the likely departure of the founder/CEO.

To remedy that, I have always encouraged companies to have the managers for each functional area present the data around their area of responsibility. Of course, this often involves hours of rehearsal, tweaking presentations, and preparing the staff members to answer questions honestly while highlighting their competence. However, a well-prepared management team performing a well-prepared management presentation not only can help seal a deal, but also often drives enhanced selling prices and stay packages.

So, the banker begins outreach, and it's time for your team to practice the presentation that is fundamentally a cut-down version of the CIM. Respective department heads will present each functional area, and the team prepares to communicate their successes and challenges to potential acquirers, highlighting your company's depth beyond its founders.

Let's say your company has taken the sage advice of its banker and brought in a consultant to help the team hone its presentation. Not that your team hasn't presented information about the company a thousand times by now, but management presentations geared toward selling a company are a different kind of important. Subtle nuances in the way questions are answered can make the difference between an offer and a pass.

A consultant will know what to look for, what to amplify, and what to avoid, and that wisdom can prove invaluable. With a consultant's help, your posse can articulate the value and potential of the company with the energy of seasoned public speakers. Coaching will help them convey enthusiasm, authenticity, and an infectious devotion to mission, while responding to questions with a transparency that inspires confidence. Note: If you're looking for such a consultant or coach, "I know a guy." Contact me.

One of the goals of these presentations is to allow the potential buyers to see that the management team works effectively together and would be a strong addition to the buyer's organization. Since human resources are a vital component of a sale, potential acquirers scrutinize the company's communications and interactions to assess whether its team is autonomous or dependent on the founders. Your company's aim at this moment is to come across as deeply, truly healthy, with all team members at once highly skilled, knowledgeable, and excitedly engaged.

When you get to this stage, all that preparation—and the years of Guardrail-driven work that preceded it—is at the brink of paying off. Your startup road trip is approaching the highway's end, and at last, the Destination is in sight.

Considering Offer Options

Assuming your team delivers a series of knockout presentations, the offers will come in. Consider this short list of three imaginary final offers—a sampling of what you may find yourself looking at when your company's time comes. Each offer has its own unique structure and implications for the team and the investors.

- Option one: An all-cash offer of $100 million, requiring founding leadership to commit to a two-year stay to receive their full payout.

- Option two: An $80 million offer from a private equity firm. In this circumstance, the PE firm acquires an 80 percent stake with management incentives tied to the remaining equity, signaling a long-term commitment from the leadership team. The remaining equity is then monetized when the PE firm sells the portfolio company, and if the business is successful, the second sale could earn the key leaders more than the initial sale.

- Option three: A $125 million cash offer from a strategic buyer, although with uncertainties about retaining your team post-acquisition.

Ethical Commitments to Employees

Now your company must negotiate with the buyer. With Ganeden, as negotiations drew to a close and we selected the buyer, there was a feeling of quiet terror. Although the team at Ganeden knew we were in a process to sell the business, only a few of us knew the details of what was about to happen. It was exciting, but we were also at a point in the journey where life was about to radically change—and that was assuming that it all went through. Could everything fall apart at the last moment? Could a natural disaster delay or stop the transaction? (I've experienced this happening, and it is not good.) Could we have stuck it out a few more years and made significantly more money (or less)? The questions were real, and they kept me up at night, for many, many nights.

You will face this wave of fear. But keeping your focus on your Guardrails—with the Destination and Goodness of the decision being key—you will move forward with stakeholder well-being in mind.

Let's envision that all three offers have met the board's minimum requirement, and shareholder approval will be easily obtained. The board discusses the options with the management team, and option three is the hands-down winner. It is now time to sit down with the acquiring company and do a complete review of all members of your team. This review will serve two purposes: first, it will familiarize the acquirers with the team, and second, it will determine who will be staying long term, who will be part of a transition team but may not stay long term, and who will not be staying. This is really important for you to do *with* the acquiring company, rather than letting them figure it out on their own (which happens far too often), as you have the ability to influence who will stay, for how long, and what type of assurances your employees would have relating to their future employment. Plus, those who do not make the cut will appreciate that you planned for their exit and soft landing. These are key decisions, and they play a pivotal role in determining how Good a transaction turns out.

If you've been resonating with this book's discussion of the Good principle in Guardrailing, particularly in the area of team building, your business will likely have anticipated this potential scenario.

Again, I believe that all employees—every single one—should have some upside when a company is sold. That upside typically comes in the form of stock options with immediate vesting at change of control. This incentivizes team members to stick around, but also shows them that the company and its investors are interested in their success as well as the success of the investment.

Additionally, I encourage you to work with your board to approve a transaction bonus for each employee—perhaps equal to six months' salary—as a way of thanking the team for their dedication to seeing the company to its Destination. This transaction bonus again shows your appreciation, and it is typically an unexpected benefit for team members.

You get the idea. As a company leader, it is within your power—and, I would argue, an aspect of your responsibility—to set up each of your employees for a positive outcome, no matter how the purchaser perceives the value of their position.

And Finally ... Destination Reached

Next comes a couple of months of intensive coordination with the acquirer's attorneys, followed by a closing call that marks the culmination of your journey. That glittering city, those towering mountain peaks, that shimmering endless sea you've been road-tripping toward: *You've arrived!* Park the car. Stretch. Let out a shriek of joy in honor of your relentless focus on this end goal.

You can pop the bubbles now. But be prepared to feel some mixed emotions.

When Ganeden finally scheduled the closing call and made it through a few stressful moments relating to last-minute details, it was done. Our company was part of the Kerry Group, and everything we had worked for over the past eleven years was left in their very capable hands. As I've told every person I've ever worked with—when you sell your company, you are no longer in control, and what happens, happens. But in the case of Ganeden, we had a strong transition plan, the folks at Kerry were very generous in the way they handled our team, and the deal was a success.

The Destination had been reached, and it was time to get out of the car and do a little dance. But I didn't feel like dancing. I felt a weird sense of numbness knowing that the following day, I would be hosting the team that would lead the integration of the companies—and knowing that I would be dealing with a host of questions and emotions from our team.

We announced the transaction to the entire company and asked them to prepare for the next day's integration meeting. Of course, there were lots and lots of questions about the transition: who was staying, who was going, what were we doing with the office and lab, etc. But the questions and concerns were softened by the transaction bonus that we gave to each employee and the payment for the stock options that they had been holding on to for all those years. Overall, there was a feeling of "we showed them" and lots of talk about how when we first started the business, the odds were against us, but we pushed through, had a blast doing it, and all made money together. It was truly a celebration.

The Integration Process

Typically, after closing, the acquiring company's management team will visit your offices and detail the way they intend to integrate the business. There will of course be changes and not all employees are likely to be promised positions that will last over the long term. But thanks to your robust negotiations, the buyer has hopefully offered generous stay packages for key staff and a predetermined severance for anyone who would eventually be let go. It's a great feeling knowing that you've secured a commitment that no one on your team will be leaving for at least the first six months while the buyer works on the integration.

Not surprisingly, with the new owner comes stark contrasts to the Guardrailing style your team is used to. After all, the business world tends to lean on familiar, if less effective, approaches. But (thanks to Guardrailing) every employee knew from the start that they would be sacrificing some of their processes when the business was sold. While the integration will have its challenges, it also signals a successful conclusion to your entrepreneurial saga.

Celebration and Reflection

It's time to celebrate with all the employees whose focus, dedication, and hard work fulfilled your collective dream. And it's time to reflect. Your leadership team may find themselves grappling with a bittersweet reality—maybe the success of the sale is tempered by the loss of what felt like a family, not just a company. Having worked within your ethical Guardrails through this process, you might now see that the value you have created extends far beyond the financial payout, and that's a poignant realization. But seller's remorse, a common sentiment, can be countered by the realization that you have not just built a business. You've also nurtured a community, one that has shared in what may be for many a once-in-a-lifetime event.

When your business reaches this point, I urge you to savor the swirl of feelings that arise. This is what you have put your whole self into, and a successful finish deserves your deepest gratification.

Successfully selling a company has the potential to change lives. Those who stay with the company may relocate, travel internationally, and experience a new corporate culture. Those who leave set out to find new opportunities using their recent success as a springboard for something bigger and better.

For me, selling Ganeden changed a few things. It gave me the freedom to decide what was important to me, as I entered into the second half of my adult life. I knew that I did not want to be an executive with a large multinational company, and I knew I wanted more flexibility in my schedule to spend more time with my family. I bought my parents a car, paid off my tiny mortgage, and set up a giving fund, but I didn't need a sports car, a mansion, or a vacation home—I was pretty happy doing just what I was doing. We stepped up the travel a bit and maybe splurged on nicer Airbnbs, but that's about the extent of the extravagance.

Guardrailing worked. It kept us on a path to the Destination while we made hundreds of Good decisions along the way. Ganeden brought good to the world, and thanks to the work Kerry is doing with BC[30], it will go on far beyond my years. And with the freedom the sale brought about, I have been able to focus on advisory work and supporting companies I felt could go down a similar path. In other words, the Ganeden achievement propelled me forward into Guardrailing on a personal level: I continue to aim for the Destination of helping worthy businesses succeed, and I make my choices based on my commitment to bringing about Good.

Reflection Questions

It's important to prepare your company along the way for this final Destination process.

- What Guardrails will you put in place to ensure your business cares for the employees who have given their time and effort to get the company to its Destination?

- What Guardrails will you be sure to hold to as you and your team make these crucial decisions?

- Who will DJ the party?

CHAPTER 11

That's a Wrap!

The majority of business owners with
a mission-driven initiative say it has a strong impact
on the overall success of their business.

—Jenn Flynn, Head of Small Business Bank at Capital One

The overview provided in this book is not a foolproof formula for success. What seems like a clear Destination, for example, is sometimes a mirage, one that you trek toward only to find that you have been chasing an idea with a fatal flaw you discovered far too late. You can give up and walk away defeated, or you can choose to accept the reality that is and move on with lessons learned and battle scars that will toughen you up for your next journey.

For those readers who work in or around the natural products industry, the good news is that you will find the community forgiving of well-intended, authentic attempts that may fall flat. It is a community of people who appreciate those who do what they say they are going to do and do those things for the greater good. In short, if at first you don't succeed, you are not alone.

No matter what field you're in, when you focus on service and keeping the best interests of all stakeholders in mind, you simply cannot go wrong. And don't forget who your stakeholders are;

they extend far beyond the investors and employees of your company. They may include consumers, retailers—online as well as brick and mortar—distributors, suppliers, and contract manufacturers, and not just investors but their partners and investors, and not just employees but their families and friends. It's a sprawling network of people whose lives are impacted by the functioning of your business. Plus, let's not forget society in general. When you start a company, you affect many people that you never consider. Even solopreneurs' businesses can affect large communities of individuals far beyond those they have ever considered. Think of all the people who benefit when a business is started, from the person who administers the system at the IRS that issues Tax IDs to new businesses, to the company you hire to clean your office, to your children, to the local barista you tip every morning.

One of the great joys of my life is helping others achieve their goals. It is thrilling to see new businesses emerge and take shape, to watch the creative minds behind them reap the benefits of their demanding work and vision. I am grateful to be in the business of helping people and that I am paid to advise, speak, and coach. At the end of the day, I am commercially motivated, but I hope that those who know me well recognize that I strive to be much more than that. Over the years, I have found that the toughest times often result in the greatest lessons, and when those challenges are overcome, they can also produce the greatest rewards.

I am one of the luckiest people on earth. I have a wonderful, supportive family, great friends, many of whom I have met working in the natural products industry, a life that allows me the flexibility to operate (mostly) on my own terms, and the joy of knowing that I am able to help people in ways that I only dreamed would be possible.

I hope one of these people is you.

Michael Bush

Michael Bush is the co-founder of GrowthWays Partners, providing strategic advisory services to entrepreneurs, founders, investors, management teams, and related stakeholders. He is passionate about optimizing the enterprise value of companies in the natural products industry while ensuring that the value they build provides benefits far beyond the financial.

With a career spanning over 25 years, Michael has led venture-backed businesses in the natural products, healthcare, and bioinformatics industries. Notably, as the president and CEO of probiotic innovator Ganeden, he expanded the market of the company's patented ingredient to over 65 countries and more than 1,000 SKUs. His tenure culminated in the successful 2017 merger with Kerry, Inc.

Michael has raised over $200 million in growth capital and participated in dozens of M&A transactions, including successful exits worth over $325 million. He speaks frequently at wellness industry events, including BevNet, Natural Products Expo, and

Supply Side. He's an investor and board member for several for-profit and not-for-profit organizations and holds degrees in Biomedical Technology and Business Administration.

Michael lives in San Francisco and is a devoted husband and father of three fabulous daughters. He enjoys his time off playing the guitar and traveling. As a certified meditation instructor, Michael is dedicated to a path of personal growth and helping others find ways to integrate mindfulness into their lives.

ACKNOWLEDGMENTS

This book would not have been possible without the incredible support of my wife, Anna Soref, my daughters, Olivia, Chloe, and Sophie, and my mother, Betty. And it certainly would never have come to fruition without the inspiration, patience, and guidance of my publisher, Modern Wisdom Press, which is led by the duo of Catherine Gregory and Nathan Joblin and their team of superstars. Additionally, I wouldn't be where I am professionally without mentors and partners, including Andy Lefkowitz, Bill Moses, Ivan and Stanley Wasserman, and countless others. This work and all that led up to it has been shaped by the challenges, failures, and successes that have created the whole of my life and is supported by my community of meditators, yogis, business gurus, musicians, and oddballs that are my world. And a special final shout-out to the people doing the splendid work at The Hoffman Process and Modern Elder Academy as they are genuinely improving lives.

THANK YOU

Dear Reader,

I thank you from the bottom of my heart for your time and interest in this book. What takes a few hours to read took decades to create, and I look forward to hearing how you are using the principles of Guardrailing in your world.

Reach out, share your experiences, and sign up to receive updates. As a gift to you, I hope you'll check out my online *Values Assessment*, where you can determine what is important to you, your company, and your world.

Go to GrowthWays.com/resources to sign up for ongoing resources and take the assessment.

Oh—and if you don't mind—please leave a review on Amazon. This will help others searching for this kind of support find this book!

To your success in work—and life.

—Mike